up where they left off, but here's what excited me most: they cracked the code on making UDL feel every bit as fun and energizing as gamification itself. For a long while, UDL felt like just another buzzword framework to check off. But Michael and John help teachers link UDL principles to incredibly engaging classroom activities in a way that finally makes sense. Reading it gave me ideas that help keep transforming my teaching in the most fun way possible.

—**Fabian Hofman,** high school teacher and co-host of *Rebel Teacher Alliance Podcast*

Playing with Purpose feels like a joyful permission slip for teachers to toss out one-size-fits-none instruction and replace it with learning experiences that actually meet the needs of every student. With UDL, gamification, and just the right dash of AI magic, classrooms can become places where curiosity wins, creativity counts, and every learner gets a seat at the table. The stories and strategies radiate the same energy I want in my own teaching—human-first, equity-driven, and fearless innovation. Matera and Meehan remind us that when teaching is rooted in play, purpose, and heart, every student can thrive.

—**Hollie Woodard,** 2022 Pennsylvania Teacher of the Year Finalist and author of *Hacking Flex Teaching*

PRAISE FOR *PLAYING WITH PURPOSE*

Playing with Purpose is a practical guide for educators who refuse to choose between joy and rigor. Matera and Meehan translate powerful pedagogy into immediately usable classroom practice, designing learning experiences that foster deep engagement, purposeful play, and sustained skill development. They present classroom experiences that are clearly grounded in contemporary educational neuroscience. Strategies that support attention, memory consolidation, and metacognitive growth are woven into every activity and assessment. I have seen how these approaches catalyze student agency and measurable learning gains. This is essential reading for school leaders and teachers committed to instruction that is both joyful and evidence-based.

—**Dr. Carl Patton,** high school principal

This book is packed with research-based strategies for building a student-centered classroom. By combining the principles of UDL with creative, high-energy lessons, John and Michael provide teachers with a practical guide for engaging all learners. This is the kind of book teachers keep on their desks, returning to it again and again for fresh ideas and renewed excitement for teaching.

—**Jamie Halsey,** fourth grade teacher and co-host of *Rebel Teacher Alliance Podcast*

Ever feel like technology is racing ahead while classrooms are trying to keep up? This book flips that script. *Playing with Purpose* shows how smart, intentional use of technology and digital tools can strengthen what happens in the classroom and open doors for every learner. It's a refreshing, practical guide for anyone who wants innovation to work with them, not against them.

—**Dr. Kimberlee Hall,** associate professor at Western Carolina University and co-author of *From Both Sides of the Desk: Faculty-Student Experiences of Effective Teaching Practices*

Playing with Purpose is a powerful anchor in a world of constant change! Michael and John aren't just authors—they are instructional design artists who masterfully take the most ordinary elements and transform them into learning masterpieces. They brilliantly equip us with the strategy, courage, and teamwork needed to not just survive but absolutely thrive in this rapidly evolving educational landscape. They effortlessly "mash up" all the best practices of student-centered learning—from UDL, which makes teaching inclusive and intentional, to gamification, which injects pure joy, creativity, and purpose into every step of the learning journey. This book isn't just helpful; it's a crucial resource that provides the immediate tools and techniques needed to bridge and close persistent learning gaps in today's learning landscape. They drive home the ultimate truth: It's not about the tool; it's about how we use it. And this book is the definitive guide to wielding those tools with clarity, precision, and purpose!

—**Dr. Jennifer Toney,** 2025 Pennsylvania Teacher of the Year Finalist

Are you ready to take the next step forward for your students? *Playing with Purpose* challenges educators to adjust their classrooms for the benefit of everyone in the room, students and teacher alike! This book takes a look at gamification through the lens of Universal Design for Learning while providing teachers with resources to help navigate this necessary change in the classroom. Michael and John do a fantastic job of explaining the how and why of UDL while also modeling the use of it with their own students and peers. When we focus on accessibility for all while celebrating our differences, everyone in the room (and world) benefits!

—**Keven Rinaman,** educator and author of *3DU: A Guide to 3D Printing in Every Classroom*

Ever since *Fully Engaged* hit the shelves, I've been eagerly anticipating another book from Michael and John. Their groundbreaking chapters on gamification and playful pedagogy—backed by solid research and easy-to-implement activity ideas—deserved a quick follow-up. And they didn't disappoint! The book you're holding picks

PLAYING WITH PURPOSE

Playing with Purpose

UNIVERSAL DESIGN FOR LEARNING IN AN AGE OF CHANGE

MICHAEL MATERA & JOHN MEEHAN

Playing with Purpose: Universal Design for Learning in an Age of Change
© 2025 Michael Matera and John Meehan

All rights reserved. No part of this publication may be reproduced in any form or by any electronic or mechanical means, including information storage and retrieval systems, without permission in writing by the publisher, except by a reviewer who may quote brief passages in a review. For information regarding permission, contact the publisher at books@daveburgessconsulting.com.

> This book is available at special discounts when purchased in quantity for educational purposes or for use as premiums, promotions, or fundraisers. For inquiries and details, contact the publisher at books@daveburgessconsulting.com.

Published by Dave Burgess Consulting, Inc.
Vancouver, WA
DaveBurgessConsulting.com

Library of Congress Control Number: 9781968898113
Paperback ISBN: 978-1-968898-11-3
Ebook ISBN: 978-1-968898-12-0

Cover and interior design by Liz Schreiter
Edited and produced by Reading List Editorial
ReadingListEditorial.com

*To the curious minds who keep us
learning, and the kindred spirits
who remind us why we play.*

CONTENTS

Introduction: The Hunger (for) Games 1

Chapter 1: Prepare to Fly: Universal Design for Learning 15
    The Candy Bar Challenge 29
    The Amazin' Online Marketplace 33
    AlphaBLAST 36

Chapter 2: Spark the Shift: Creativity and Playful Inspiration 41
    Coins for Content 61
    Swatch What Happens 64
    Caveman Grammar 66

Chapter 3: Teach with Heart: Connection in a Tech-Driven World ... 71
    Get to Know Me Empathy Maps 90
    Storytelling with Scrabble 93
    Sticker Swag Soiree 96

Chapter 4: Play with Purpose: Gamification as a
Learning Flywheel 101
    Resource Rumble 119
    Save Our Students 122
    Collab Collect 125

Chapter 5: Empower Their Choices: Voice, Autonomy,
and Motivation 131
    Double-Bubble Balancing Act 146
    Pyramid Pass and Dash 149
    Twelve-Topic Stitch-Up 153

Chapter 6: Lead the Machine: AI, Automation, and
Educator Judgment 159
    Happy Green Boxes 175
    Pokévolve Trading Card Creator 178
    Hexagon Hunters 181

Chapter 7: Cultivate the Good: Equity, Empathy, and Ethics 187
    Coin Crashers 200
    Desert Island Dilemma 204
    AI Artwork Anarchy 208

Chapter 8: Fuel the Journey: Lifelong Learning and
Lasting Curiosity 213
    Imagination Station 229
    Out of Sorts 232
    Schoolhouse Rock Stars 234

Epilogue: Savor Every Moment 239

About the Authors 242
More from Dave Burgess Consulting, Inc. 244

MAY THE ODDS BE EVER IN YOUR FAVOR.

— SUZANNE COLLINS —

INTRODUCTION

THE HUNGER (FOR) GAMES

This is not a book about technology.

In the words of Seymour Papert, the South African–born MIT mathematician, computer scientist, and pioneer in educational technology: "Technology is anything that was invented after you were born. Everything else is just stuff."

It's a sentiment that speaks to how quickly humans adapt to innovation. New tools can feel intimidating at first—disruptive even—but over time, they gradually and inevitably weave into the fabric of our daily lives. As Alan Kay, creator of the world's first tablet computer (way back in 1968!) aptly said: "That's why we don't argue anymore about whether the piano is corrupting music with technology."

From the printing press to the piano to AI-powered apps, technology has always been a double-edged sword—capable of incredible transformation but requiring thoughtful adoption by the people who use it. The key, it seems, is neither to resist change outright nor to simply embrace whatever new tech comes our way. Instead, we must learn how we, as humans, can wield these new tools with clarity, precision, and purpose.

Without question, technology amplifies the awesome and shapes the possibilities of what we can do with all the "stuff" we have at our disposal to play with. But it's the very concept of play that makes all learning possible in the first place. And far beyond the occasional "Fun Friday" approach to teaching and learning, the authors of the book you now hold in your hands wholeheartedly believe that technology can enable a much better way to play in our classrooms.

In the pages ahead, we invite you to join us in rethinking what's possible—to spark curiosity, inspire creativity, and enhance all sorts of human connections, no matter what "stuff" the future brings our way. We firmly believe that purposeful play has the power to inject meaning, wonder, curiosity, and joy into *everything* we do in our schools. And pairing these timeless elements with the clear and actionable principles of the Universal Design for Learning (UDL) framework can help today's educators take advantage of cutting-edge tools, hands-on instructional techniques, and high-impact teaching strategies to ensure that every student feels empowered to engage and succeed in the face of unprecedented change.

Every. Single. Day.

Microsoft founder Bill Gates would probably know a thing or two about the subject of transformation and the incredible impact a single change can have. This is why we couldn't help but take note of his March 2023 blog post titled "The Age of AI Has Begun." In it, he shared the story of how he challenged the developers at OpenAI to train an AI capable of passing the AP Biology exam—a test designed to assess not just factual recall but critical thinking. Gates expected this to take years, but the team succeeded in mere months.[1]

Say hello to ChatGPT—a game changer if there ever was one.

Yet this is still not a book about technology.

It's about what happens next.

This breakthrough wasn't just about technology; it underscored a profound question for education: If AI can master complex academic tasks so quickly, what does that mean for how we teach students to think critically and creatively?

What happens next isn't about the tools themselves—it's about the very real and very human purpose that we bring to them. At its heart, this book is about leveraging innovation to inspire human connection and creativity in our classrooms. And we must do so now, at this specific time, in a profession where the only constant feels like endless change. Our classrooms need strategy, courage, and teamwork to thrive in a rapidly changing landscape. To be honest, it's reminiscent of *The Hunger Games*.

But let's look back before we look ahead. In the early 1900s, electricity took thirteen years to reach mass adoption in the United States. A century later, social media giants like Facebook and Twitter hit a million users in about a year. ChatGPT? It crossed that million-user mark in less than a week, and it has since rolled out the welcome mat for upward of 699 million additional users. We're talking about seismic change—like waking up to find every textbook was replaced by TikTok tutorials overnight.

This isn't just a new trend. It's the new normal. And the implications for our classrooms are enormous. Today's kindergarteners will graduate into a workforce in 2050, live through AI-driven revolutions, and retire around 2090. The cutting-edge tech of today will be their quaint and forgotten MySpace of tomorrow.

---

1   Bill Gates, "The Age of AI Has Begun," *Gates Notes* (blog), March 21, 2023, https://www.gatesnotes.com/The-Age-of-AI-Has-Begun.

So the real question isn't if AI will reshape education. It's how we choose to respond. Education stands at a crossroads. Do we let technology dictate how we teach? Or do we harness it to amplify the timeless human elements that make teaching so powerful?

Because this isn't a book about technology. It's a book about teaching.

Tech will always change. But great teaching is timeless.

We're not chasing flashy breakthroughs or adopting AI-powered tools just because they exist. A hammer sees every problem as a nail—but we aren't looking to swing mindlessly at every new innovation. Instead, we must use these tools with intention, ensuring they serve the true purpose of our profession instead of becoming just another unnecessary burden.

Much like the revolutionary breakthroughs that defined previous eras, AI's dramatic arrival presents an opportunity. This technology can be not a replacement but a reinforcement of what matters most.

While technology can be transformative, it's the timeless principles of engagement, representation, and expression—the very pillars of UDL—that ensure these tools enrich rather than replace the human elements of education.

And at the heart of it all? Play.

Play isn't just children's work; it's the foundation for meaningful exploration and discovery at every age. And as we'll soon see, it's also one of the most powerful tools we have to make learning unforgettable for everyone.

GREAT TEACHING STARTS WITH GOOD PEOPLE

Traditional professional development leaves a lot to be desired. Too often, it's a case of "Do as I say, not as I do." Tired teachers are crammed into crowded cafeterias while a highly paid "sage on the stage"—a complete outsider to you and your colleagues—is brought in to deliver a one-size-fits-all slideshow about everything you're supposedly doing wrong in your job.

At best, it's ineffective. At worst, it's kind of insulting.

And perhaps not surprisingly, research shows that very little of what's taught at these one-shot workshops makes its way into classrooms. Industry experts estimate an implementation rate of less than 10 percent.[2]

Less than 10 percent, y'all. When teachers are expected to navigate lightning-fast technological shifts and adapt to all kinds of new paradigms that shape the way our students think, learn, and engage with the ever-changing world around them, a 10 percent success rate just doesn't cut it.

Like you, we're working teachers. We've sat through those endless PD sessions, too, questioning if this was really the best use of our time—or if it all could have just been an email. And we've encountered more than our fair share of questionable tech solutions, all promising to revolutionize education if we'd just hand over the keys to our classrooms and trust the latest newfangled website to work its AI magic.

But we don't need to make learning magical. We need to make it meaningful.

And that starts by playing with purpose.

Now more than ever, it truly feels like the entire education system is at a turning point. Nearly one in eight teaching positions in the US is unfilled or filled by someone underqualified—a challenge worsened by the pandemic and the rise of AI.[3] Access to high-quality instructional materials has become a chaotic mix of inequity and unclear policies, leaving teachers to fumble their way through the matrix of solution-peddling edtech giants, coldly automated systems of plagiarism

---

[2] Valerie Strauss, "Why Most Professional Development for Teachers Is Useless," *The Washington Post*, March 1, 2024, https://www.washingtonpost.com/news/answer-sheet/wp/2014/03/01/why-most-professional-development-for-teachers-is-useless/.

[3] Tiffany S. Tan, Ivett Arellano, and Susan Kemper Patrick, *State Teacher Shortages 2024 Update* (Learning Policy Institute, 2024), https://learningpolicyinstitute.org/media/4412/download?inline&file=State_Vacancy_2024_RESOURCE.pdf.

checkers, and AI-powered sentinels of student surveillance. Burnout is at an all-time high, leaving schools scrambling for solutions when they're needed most.

As the cool kids say, "The struggle is real."

The rapid evolution of AI tools and tech policies has brought education to a crossroads. The age of artificial intelligence isn't coming—it's already here. Our classrooms need high-quality resources. Our schools need passionate, prepared teachers. And this crisis screams for big changes and bold ideas.

So where do your humble authors fit into all of this?

As we said, we're both working educators—just like you. Michael is a veteran sixth-grade history teacher in Milwaukee, Wisconsin, balancing life as a loving dad to his teenage daughter with his passion for making learning unforgettable. John, after more than a decade teaching high school English, now works behind the scenes as an instructional coach near Washington, DC, helping teachers bring playful pedagogy to life. And as a new dad himself—his first daughter was born in March 2025—he's discovering a whole new world of learning himself.

In 2021, we cowrote *Fully Engaged: Playful Pedagogy for Real Results*, combining forces after the individual successes of Michael's *Explore Like a Pirate* (2015) and John's *EDrenaline Rush* (2019). Together, these three books offered more than two hundred unique resources to help teachers bring playful pedagogy into their classrooms. Inspired to take things even further, we launched EMC² Learning—an education platform designed to empower educators worldwide to reclaim, not replace, their creativity.

Named after one of our all-time favorite teacher heroes (more on that guy in just a moment), EMC² Learning has grown into a thriving online community. To date, we've welcomed more than ten thousand member teachers from schools around the globe and shared thousands of activities to help make learning more engaging and impactful.

At EMC² Learning, we don't provide rigid blueprints or scripts—we offer tools and templates designed to spark creativity and flexibility. In this book, you'll hear the stories of some of the phenomenal teachers we've had the honor of connecting with along the way. Best of all? No uninspired worksheets. No crass simulations. No frantic button-mashing contests. And no low-level guessing games.

Our resources are grounded in research, and in everything we design, we strive to create playful ways for teachers to turn big-picture educational theory into hands-on classroom practice. Because as it turns out, playing with purpose isn't just a passing fad in education—it's a tale as old as time.

In 1962, the journal *Childhood Education* published an article titled "Play Is Education" by N. V. Scarfe that contained the following passage:

> All play is associated with intense thought activity and rapid intellectual growth.
>
> The highest form of research is essentially play. Einstein is quoted as saying, "The desire to arrive finally at logically connected concepts is the emotional basis of a vague play with basic ideas. This combinatory or associative play seems to be the essential feature in productive thought."[4]

Noted child psychologist Jean Piaget dedicated his life's work to studying the importance of play in the foundational stages of children's intellectual development. Education reformers like Maria Montessori made it their mission to create playful, self-guided spaces where children could learn and grow through curiosity and wonder. And longtime children's television pioneer Mr. Rogers famously once remarked that "play is often talked about as if it were a relief from serious learning. But for children, play is serious learning. Play is really the work of childhood."

Einstein. Piaget. Montessori. Mr. Rogers.

And then there's us.

While we can't quite claim the brilliance of these icons of creative thought, we do know a thing or two about teaching, learning, and playing with purpose. At EMC² Learning—which we named in Einstein's honor—we like to say that engagement moves at the speed of life. And we've helped thousands of teachers bring this same playful spin on Einstein's most famous maxim to life in classrooms worldwide.

In a world of constant change, curiosity remains our anchor. It bridges the gap between cutting-edge tools and timeless teaching practices, transforming new technologies like AI from intimidating disruptors into empowering partners in learning. Just as crayons and LEGO bricks spark creativity, a playful spirit can unlock the potential of any tool—no matter how high-tech it might be.

---

4   N. V. Scarfe, "Play is Education," *Childhood Education* 39, no. 3 (1962): 117–121.

Since launching our site to coincide with the release of *Fully Engaged* in 2021, we've created more than a thousand classroom activities designed to inspire students and sustain teachers' joy for their craft. Guided by UDL principles, we tinker, test, and refine teaching strategies that balance critical thinking with student-friendly appeal. And in the pages ahead, we're sharing the best of what we've built—ready for you to play with, adapt, and make your own.

Because let's face it: You can't write four books on fifty ways to give a kid a sticker.

LET'S CHANGE THE GAME

From AI-assisted lesson plans to ever-shifting standards, today's educators are navigating a world that moves faster than ever. In a profession where it can feel like the only constant is change, knowing where to begin isn't always easy. That's why this book is built to shift the conversation from uncertainty to action. Instead of getting lost in the chaos, we'll explore how to respond with purpose, flexibility, and a healthy dose of play.

Each chapter centers on a single call to action—a rallying cry for teachers ready to meet change head on without losing sight of what matters most: students, connection, and curiosity. Whether you're designing more inclusive lessons, experimenting with game-based strategies, or wrestling with the ethics of emerging technologies, you'll find practical tools, inspiring insights, and ready-to-use ideas to help you adapt and thrive.

So let's change the game. One chapter at a time.

Chapter 1
Prepare to Fly: Universal Design for Learning

Step boldly into the world of UDL, where intentional flexibility and inclusivity ensure that every student is empowered to thrive—no matter where they're starting from.

Chapter 2
Spark the Shift: Creativity and Playful Inspiration

Discover how the smallest spark of creativity can ignite transformative learning experiences, fostering joy, curiosity, and innovation in your classroom.

Chapter 3
Teach with Heart: Connection in a Tech-Driven World

Explore the deeply human side of education and learn how to balance digital tools with the empathy and presence that make teaching matter.

Chapter 4
Play with Purpose: Gamification as a Learning Flywheel

Harness the power of game-based learning to build engagement, increase rigor, and unlock the hero within every student.

Chapter 5
Empower Their Choices: Voice, Autonomy, and Motivation

Meaningful choice is the engine of mastery. Learn how to build classroom systems that promote autonomy while still guiding students toward growth.

Chapter 6
Lead the Machine: AI, Automation, and Educator Judgment

With humor, humility, and hard-won lessons, we explore the ups, downs, and limits of educational technology—and how to stay human in a world full of bots.

Chapter 7
Cultivate the Good: Equity, Empathy, and Ethics

Navigate the moral maze of education with strategies to foster inclusion, promote justice, and strengthen your classroom community.

Chapter 8
Fuel the Journey: Lifelong Learning and Lasting Curiosity

Put the playful pedagogy pedal to the metal and rediscover what it means to teach, learn, and grow with purpose—even as the world keeps changing around you.

You don't need to master everything overnight. And you definitely don't need to be perfect. But as educators, we do need to keep showing up—curious, courageous, and willing to try something new.

Ready, Player One?

Oh yeah. One last thing...

FROM PLAYFUL RESEARCH TO PRACTICAL RESOURCES

We know that teachers are hungry for high-quality resources and ideas that will engage, inspire, sustain, and support them in the amazing work they do. And we know that our students are just as hungry for classroom activities that help them become authentically engaged in whatever they're learning about, no matter where they live or what age they are.

We believe that students should not be audience members to their own learning. And our goal in writing this book is to help get them back in the game.

As you make your way through the pages ahead, you'll notice that each chapter wraps up with a power-packed playbook—a curated collection of gamified teaching activities designed to help you put the chapter's big ideas into practice. It might help to approach these playbooks like your very own teacher tool kit: They're here to make your life as a modern educator easier and more exciting, providing plug-and-play ideas that are quick to implement and endlessly adaptable.

And the best part? Every single resource in this book has been intentionally designed to be content agnostic. So all you'll have to do is pick a playbook suggestion of your choice, add a sprinkle of your curriculum (or a splash of AI), and the activity is ready to go!

Here's what you can expect from every resource you'll find in the playbooks ahead:

- **Quick-start guide:** Each resource begins with a quick and clear explanation of the activity, giving you everything you need to get started right away. Think of it as your blueprint for success, with step-by-step instructions to guide the way.
- **Pedagogy power-up:** This is where we take a moment to connect the dots between your existing pedagogy and these playful upgrades. Whether the activity is a fresh twist on a familiar concept or a brand-new approach, these tips will show you how it can seamlessly enhance teaching practices you already know by heart.
- **House rules:** Every classroom is unique, and the best activities are the ones that adapt to fit your students' needs. In this section, you'll find creative tweaks and variations to make the activity your own—maybe by adjusting the rules for timing, group size, or tools at your disposal. Want to add a tech-friendly twist or supercharge things with artificial intelligence? We've

got ideas for leveraging AI tools where they fit naturally to take things to the next level.
- **UDL for the win:** Finally, we'll highlight how each activity aligns with Universal Design for Learning principles, ensuring that it's engaging, accessible, and adaptable for all your students.

As much as possible, we've tried to balance each chapter with equal measures of big-picture research and hands-on teaching techniques that can help make your instruction more joyful, more purposeful, and more impactful at every step along the way. Flip ahead, dive in, and let's start *Playing with Purpose* together!

ONE OF MY FAVORITE PHOBIAS IS THAT GIRLS, ESPECIALLY THOSE WHOSE TASTES AREN'T ROUTINE, OFTEN DON'T GET A FAIR BREAK . . .

—— AMELIA EARHART ——

CHAPTER 1

PREPARE TO FLY

UNIVERSAL DESIGN FOR LEARNING

In the 1950s, the US Air Force faced a devastating crisis: Despite piloting the world's most advanced fighter jets, young pilots were dying at an alarming rate, with dozens of aircraft crashing weekly. Frazzled commanders scrambled for answers, suspecting flaws in their equipment, training protocols, or even the pilots themselves.

But the truth was far stranger—and deadlier.

The cockpits of US fighter jets had been designed in the 1920s using the "average" dimensions of pilots at the time. By the 1950s, those averages were woefully out of date. In response, army engineers painstakingly remeasured thousands of modern servicemen to create what they hoped would be the ultimate one-size-fits-all upgrade in cockpit design.

Yet something still wasn't working.

Of the four thousand pilots measured, not a single one fit the so-called average dimensions across the board. Some were slightly taller or wider, broader or thinner, with arms or fingertips just a fraction longer or shorter than those of their peers. And at speeds exceeding seven hundred miles per hour with pilots soaring some fifty thousand feet in the air, even the smallest mismatch could have catastrophic consequences—controls out of reach, poorly placed restraints, and deadly delays.

Enter Lt. Gilbert Daniels, a young Harvard graduate with a background not in aeronautics but anthropology. Tasked with analyzing the data behind cockpit designs, Daniels asked a bold question: What if the average doesn't exist? His meticulous analysis revealed a groundbreaking insight—designing for an imaginary "average pilot" unintentionally excluded everyone. In trying to build for the average, they had overlooked the individual at a terrible cost.

Daniels proposed a radical solution: adjustable cockpits. Instead of a one-size-fits-all design, engineers would create customizable settings—seats, straps, controls, and more—that could be tailored to each airman. Initially dismissed as impractical and expensive, the idea gained traction due to desperation. The results were astonishing. The accident rate plummeted. Destroyed aircraft per one hundred thousand flying hours dropped from approximately 23.6 in the 1950s to 4.3 in the 1960s, then to just 2.3 by the 1970s.[5]

With these simple accommodations now the new industry standard, pilots of all shapes and sizes could finally operate their aircraft safely and effectively, saving countless lives and revolutionizing aviation forever.

Spoiler: This story isn't just about fighter jets.

In fact, the lesson Lt. Daniels uncovered—that designing for the margins creates better outcomes for everyone—applies just as powerfully

---

[5] Thomas Light, Thomas Hamilton, and Spencer Pfeifer, *Trends in U.S. Air Force Aircraft Mishap Rates (1950–2018)* (Rand Corporation, 2020), https://www.rand.org/content/dam/rand/pubs/research_reports/RRA200/RRA257-1/RAND_RRA257-1.pdf.

to education. Much like pilots, students come with a wide range of needs, abilities, and strengths that cannot be addressed by a one-size-fits-all approach. Designing for the so-called average student risks excluding everyone, while adaptive, inclusive systems unlock opportunities for all learners to thrive.

It's a powerful reminder of individual variability—a universal truth that applies to learning as much as aviation. No matter how advanced or high-tech our systems may seem, designing for the "average" often fails to meet the needs of the very individuals we aim to support. In classrooms, students bring a rich diversity of skills, backgrounds, and needs, challenging us to design learning environments that provide multiple pathways to success. Lt. Daniels's insight prompts us to answer these questions: Are we building educational systems that accommodate this variability, using multiple means of engagement to meet students where they are? Or are we still building for an imaginary "average student," leaving far too many learners to fend for themselves as they prepare to face the inevitable standardized testing machine?

To wit: Are we building our classrooms for *something*? Or are we building our classrooms for *someone*?

In education, like aviation, designing for the "average" often means excluding everyone. To honor the diversity of our classrooms, we need to level the playing field by creating flexible systems that adapt to the unique strengths and challenges of each learner. In an age of rapid technological advancement and AI-assisted learning, this is even more pressing. When educational systems are built on outdated assumptions—or blindly automated without intentional design—they can scale inequity instead of solving it.

Let's begin this chapter with a thoughtful look at the systems that form the foundation of our educational practice—especially as technology continues to evolve and reshape the way we teach and learn. Then, perhaps it's time to consider pressing the reset button. We need to change the game before everybody gets played.

GIVE A HOOT (SORRY, KAHOOT!)

Thankfully, we've come a long way in moving beyond one-size-fits-all education. Project-based learning. Differentiated instruction. Flexible seating. Student choice. These shifts have started to change how we think about content delivery—replacing rigid systems with models that honor creativity, collaboration, and critical thinking.

Still, for all the innovation that's reshaped our lesson plans, there's one staple of the classroom experience that's stuck in the past: the perennial review game.

Which leads us to a rather touchy subject . . .

Folks. We need to talk about Kahoot!

In the quest to make learning more fun, it's easy to turn to flashy review games. With prebuilt quizzes, leaderboard flair, and a $1.72 billion valuation (thanks, Goldman Sachs) it's no wonder platforms like Kahoot! are everywhere. For teachers, they're fast and easy. For students, they're bright, competitive, and loud.[6]

It's kind of like a school-friendly spin on pub trivia—minus the mozzarella sticks.

And honestly? That's part of the problem.

Now don't get us wrong. These games are a ton of fun! When used strategically, they can absolutely spark energy in the classroom as students compete with their peers and race to lock in the right answers.

The trouble comes when we stop there. Racing through shallow trivia questions is the academic equivalent of feeding kids greasy fast-food burgers and then wondering why their stomachs hurt. Flashy, fast, and fun? Sure. But it's not the kind of learning that sustains or strengthens students for what's ahead.

While these tools bring energy, they also raise a deeper question: Are we chasing excitement or designing for learning that lasts—learning that goes deeper than surface-level recall?

---

6   Ingrid Lunden, "Gamified E-learning Platform Kahoot Gets $1.7B Acquisition Offer from Goldman Sachs, Lego and more," Tech Crunch, July 14, 2023, https://techcrunch.com/2023/07/14/kahoot-acquired/.

Because here's the thing: Classroom games have the potential to be so much more than buzzer battles and bragging rights. At their core, great games are about problem-solving, experimentation, and discovery. And when paired with the transformative power of technology, they can become personalized learning experiences that push the boundaries of what's possible. The best games adapt to individual learners, offer meaningful feedback, and spark the kind of creative thinking that goes far beyond simple recall.

But (and this is a pretty big "but") . . . this only happens when we broaden our understanding of gaming in the classroom. It's not about the tool; it's about how we use it. It's about designing opportunities for students to explore, innovate, and engage deeply with content.

That means ditching the sugar rush and designing for serious engagement.

So let's dig into the scoreboard and explore how we can play with purpose in ways that engage every learner and stand the test of change.

THE SCOREBOARD TELLS THE TALE

There's an old Moroccan proverb that reminds us to "love truth even if it harms you, and hate lies even if they serve you."[7]

Well buckle up, gang, because we're about to drop a payload of truth bombs. And this one is going to hurt.

In buzzer-style games like the one illustrated on the sample scoreboard that follows, the excitement of competition can sometimes overshadow the focus on meaningful learning. On the surface, these games are fun, fast-paced, and full of energy—and they're often accompanied by detailed CSV reports that boast a play-by-play breakdown of each player's performance.

But let's pause for a moment to read between the lines and see how our sample students actually fared:

---

7 "Proverbs—Common Sayings Used in Morocco," Morocco.com, accessed September 23, 2025, https://www.morocco.com/culture/moroccan-proverbs/.

SCOREBOARD	
Bobby ButtonMasher	904 ↑
Susie Knowsherstuff	783 ↑
Lucky Guess Larry	645
AverageJOE	540
Reid Ing Closely	480
cixelsyD ynnaD	440
x10did Thyme	0

- Bobby ButtonMasher: Hooray for locking in first place! But speed shouldn't trump thoughtfulness. Games that reward quick reflexes exclude students who need more time to process. Sure, Bobby's quick today, but button mashing won't build the grit he'll need for tackling complex, time-intensive challenges tomorrow.
- Susie Knowsherstuff: Celebrating "top" performers while leaving others behind erodes morale and creates fixed mindsets on both sides. Students start believing they either have the right stuff or they don't—a mindset that fuels pressure and even cheating, especially in honors and AP classes.
- Lucky Guess Larry: Guessing games cheapen learning. Unless we replace trivia questions with challenges that require reasoning and creativity, luck will keep outweighing understanding—and students will win or lose by a coin flip. That's a bad break for all parties involved.
- AverageJOE: Middle performers often get overlooked in competitive games. Even if they've got a pretty good handle

on what's being asked of them, we keep asking it again and again in the exact same fashion, and that hardly gives them the opportunity to expand their understanding or try to make sense of that familiar information in new and surprising ways.
- Reid Ing Closely: Countdown timers can lead to rushing, which penalizes those students who actually take the time to read things carefully. Worse, every buzzer game reinforces the very same shrinking, TikTok-sized attention spans that teachers lament—fueling reward-chasing habits instead of thoughtful engagement.
- cixelsyD ynnaD: This username may look like gibberish at first blush, but read it backward from right to left—it's Dyslexic Danny. Imagine being a student with the most common learning disability on the planet, struggling to decode a question as the timer ticks down.[8] By the time they process it, the game moves on, leaving frustration and shame in its wake.
- x10did Thyme: Rounding out our fictional crew of student gamers, we see a user by the name of x10did Thyme. While time constraints can push some students to excel, they can likewise leave others—including many with IEPs—utterly paralyzed by anxiety. If every game we play fails to account for flexible timing options to help our classrooms strike that balance between excitement and inclusivity, we're simply not giving every student a fair shot at success.

The bottom line?

Kahoot!, Gimkit, Blooket, you name it—though they might still be the industry standard, buzzer-style games have troubling design flaws. A great classroom game celebrates diverse strengths and embraces multiple means of engagement by ensuring all students feel included and capable of contributing. By fostering collaboration over competition

---

[8] "The Top 5 Most Common Learning Disabilities & Their Symptoms," LD Resources Foundation Action, accessed September 23, 2025, https://www.ldrfa.org/the-top-5-most-common-learning-disabilities-their-symptoms.

and intentionally designing with individual variability in mind, educators can create experiences that resonate with every learner. If we aren't designing instruction to offer flexible opportunities for participation and success, we risk leaving too many students behind, reinforcing barriers instead of breaking them down.

But before we dive into all the fun possibilities of meaningful gaming, there's one more big barrier we need to break down together.

"LEARNING STYLES" AREN'T ACTUALLY A THING

We're not sure why this myth lingers, but let's settle this once and for all, shall we?

As Olga Khazan wrote in *The Atlantic*, "A popular theory that some people learn better visually or aurally keeps getting debunked."[9] The American Psychological Association called it out directly in 2019, stating that believing in the learning styles myth may be detrimental.[10] Or as psychologists Cedar Riener and Daniel Willingham put it succinctly in 2010: "There is no credible evidence that learning styles exist."[11]

Here's the truth: Students may prefer certain ways of learning, but there's zero evidence that catering to those preferences actually improves outcomes.

Learner variability is real, within individuals and across groups, but "learning styles" as a framework? It's time to move on. There's a better, research-backed way to reach every student: Universal Design for Learning.

Let's break it down step by step.

---

9 Olga Khazan, "The Myth of 'Learning Styles,'" *The Atlantic*, April 11, 2018, https://www.theatlantic.com/science/archive/2018/04/the-myth-of-learning-styles/557687/.

10 American Psychological Association, "Belief in Learning Styles Myth May Be Detrimental," May 30, 2019, press release, https://www.apa.org/news/press/releases/2019/05/learning-styles-myth.

11 Patrick Carroll, "Leaning Styles Don't Actually Exist, Studies Show," Foundation for Economic Education, August 12, 2022, https://fee.org/articles/learning-styles-don-t-actually-exist-studies-show.

UDL is more than an educational buzzword; it's a game-changing approach rooted in a simple principle: Design for the margins, and everyone benefits.

Borrowed from the world of architecture (think of curb cuts like the one pictured below, originally for wheelchair users but now helpful for parents with strollers, travelers with suitcases, and more), UDL removes barriers in education by offering flexible, inclusive options that benefit *all* learners.

At its core, UDL aligns with how the brain works, focusing on three principles:

- **Engagement** (the *why* of learning): Motivate students by offering choices that reflect their interests, needs, and values. When learning feels personal, walls come down and curiosity takes hold.

- **Representation** (the *what* of learning): Present content in diverse ways—text, visuals, audio, or hands-on tasks—so every student can access it in a way that makes sense to them.
- **Action and expression** (the *how* of learning): Provide flexible options for students to show what they've learned. Have them write, speak, draw, create, or code. Flexibility empowers students to demonstrate mastery their own way.

Just as curb cuts transformed our physical spaces, UDL transforms classrooms into places where every learner can thrive. It's a framework to optimize teaching and learning for all people, and it's based on scientific insights into how humans learn. Fittingly, UDL's origins trace back to 1984, a year marked by two major shifts: a renewed focus on school reform and (yup, you guessed it) the rise of personal computers like the Macintosh.[12]

That same year, a group of education researchers founded CAST (formerly the Center for Applied Special Technology). Their mission? To explore how new technologies could improve learning for students with disabilities. Over time, their work evolved into a flexible, inclusive framework: Universal Design for Learning.

Today, CAST continues to lead the charge, applying UDL to curriculum design, teacher preparation, policy, and more. Their message remains clear: When we design for diverse needs, we don't just support students who struggle; we level the playing field for *everyone*.

Great design doesn't just remove barriers. It unlocks opportunities for creativity, collaboration, and critical thinking to thrive.

And that, in a nutshell, is the heart of UDL.

But here's the challenge: While UDL offers a powerful framework, turning it into everyday classroom practice can feel daunting. That's where playful pedagogy—a technique called gamification—comes into our instructional designer's tool kit. Gamification adds a layer of

---

12 CAST, "Timeline of Innovation," December 5, 2024, https://www.cast.org/impact/timeline-innovation.

engagement and joy, transforming lessons into experiences that align seamlessly with UDL's principles.

We'll explore gamification more closely in chapter 4, but here's the key takeaway: By weaving playful, gamelike techniques into our lessons, we can bring UDL to life and engage every learner while making the learning process more joyful, accessible, and meaningful. For now, let's take a quick look at how a playful approach can make UDL not just achievable but irresistible.

ENGAGEMENT

Gamified elements like choice, narrative, and progress tracking ignite curiosity and give students a sense of purpose. Think about how leaderboards, challenges, or role-playing missions turn passive learners into active participants. Small, playful tweaks to our existing pedagogy hook students by meeting them where they are—curious, playful, and eager to explore. By tying engagement to meaningful goals, we build the *why* behind learning.

In our classrooms, this might look like the following:

- **Choice boards as adventure maps:** Present a choice board of activities as a game map where students select their "quests," giving them autonomy over their learning path.
- **Narrative-driven warm-ups:** Start a lesson with a story-driven scenario that connects to the day's objectives and activates prior knowledge. Add a choose-your-own-adventure twist to turn routine tasks into immersive missions.
- **Systems of points and rewards:** Move beyond games that reward speed over skill. Award points for effort, collaboration, or creativity, emphasizing intrinsic motivation and teamwork over competition.

REPRESENTATION

Games thrive on diversity—offering players multiple ways to access information and solve problems. The same principles apply when gamifying our lessons. We can look for opportunities to present our content visually, verbally, or through any means of hands-on exploration. By incorporating diverse entry points into learning, we ensure every student has a way to get in the game. By connecting them with the material, we foster accessibility and facilitate deeper understanding.

In our classrooms, this might look like the following:

- **Visual storytelling:** Use game cards, digital avatars, or infographic-style visuals to explain key concepts, helping students visualize and contextualize information.
- **Collaborative problem-solving challenges:** Introduce escape room–style activities where students decode clues using textual, auditory, and visual inputs, encouraging teamwork and leveraging multiple modes of learning.
- **Interactive simulations:** Engage students with virtual models, historical reenactments, or gamified science experiments that allow them to manipulate variables and see immediate results.

ACTION AND EXPRESSION

In games, players aren't judged by how they follow one path to success but by the creative ways they solve problems. Playful pedagogy with a UDL focus embraces this same flexibility, offering students multiple ways to demonstrate their understanding. By moving beyond those clunky and outdated one-size-fits-all assessments, we empower students to show their mastery in ways that reflect their unique strengths and creativity.

In our classrooms, this might look like the following:

- **Gamelike assessments:** Replace traditional quizzes with challenges where students "level up" by completing creative tasks, work together with peers to win an epic "boss battle" inspired by your curriculum, or solve progressively harder problems, integrating the assessment into their daily learning flow.
- **Role-playing presentations:** Have students embody historical figures, scientists, or literary characters to present findings or argue perspectives, turning presentations into immersive, memorable experiences.
- **Digital portfolios as player profiles:** Encourage students to build digital portfolios that track their progress over time, like a player profile in a game. Include badges, achievements, and evidence of their growth across multiple areas.

UDL gives us the blueprint for creating classrooms where every learner can thrive, while gamification provides the spark to make that vision a reality. Together, they form a dynamic duo: UDL ensures our teaching is inclusive and intentional, while gamification injects joy, creativity, and purpose into every step of the learning journey.

This isn't about isolated games or one-off activities—it's about transforming the way we teach, making every stage of instruction feel like an invitation to play, explore, and grow. By weaving these two frameworks together, we create spaces where all students can engage meaningfully, access content on their terms, and express their learning in ways that feel authentic and empowering.

So are you ready to change the game?

Instead of offering a collection of stand-alone activities for a specific subject area or high-level theories, everything that follows in this book is designed to help you bridge the gap—turning UDL into practical, gamelike strategies that fit seamlessly into your teaching flow regardless of what you teach. These are tools designed not just for "Fun Friday" but for every stage of learning, becoming an integral part of every student's learning journey.

Because when we design for the margins and infuse our lessons with joy, we're not just helping students master the curriculum—we're helping them discover what they're truly capable of.

A PLAYBOOK FOR UNIVERSAL DESIGN

Engagement is the cornerstone of effective teaching. When we design lessons that actively engage our students, we create an environment where students learn meaningfully, not passively.

And this doesn't just pertain to the classroom.

Between the aftershocks of the pandemic and the rise of AI, engagement in our schools and workplaces is at an all-time low. In the face of such monumental change, it seems that an overwhelming majority of folks across all walks of life are living through a sort of professional crisis of purpose. In fact, Gallup reports only 32 percent of US workers feel engaged, with young people feeling especially disconnected, unheard, and undervalued.[13]

Sound familiar?

Just like adults, students need someone who believes in them, supports their growth, and makes learning meaningful. That's what UDL does. By prioritizing engagement, providing diverse options for representation, and offering multiple means of action and expression, we shift the conversation. "What's the matter with you?" becomes "What matters to you?"

Different students learn in different ways on different days. And when we remove systemic barriers in our schools so that all students are encouraged to learn in whatever way makes sense to them, learning becomes a lifelong pursuit, not just a classroom obligation.

---

13 Andrea Hsu, "America, We Have a Problem. People Aren't Feeling Engaged with Their Work," Houston Public Media, January 25, 2023, https://www.houstonpublicmedia.org/npr/2023/01/25/1150816271/america-we-have-a-problem-people-arent-feeling-engaged-with-their-work/.

The activities in this section are your springboard to designing lessons that engage, motivate, and empower your students. By embracing the principles of UDL and creating flexible, inclusive systems, we can transform our classrooms into spaces where every learner feels seen, valued, and inspired to thrive—because every student deserves a chance to shine.

THE CANDY BAR CHALLENGE

Game On
Let your students enjoy the sweet fun of free association with the Candy Bar Challenge! Without needing a single piece of candy, this activity inspires students to write as many creative, content-driven sentences as possible, incorporating famous candy names into their answers. This lighthearted challenge sharpens their content knowledge while adding a playful twist to any lesson.

A Universal Upgrade
Instead of rote recaps and traditional writing prompts, this activity engages students' creativity, sharpens content knowledge, and encourages collaboration—all while incorporating UDL principles of engagement, representation, and action and expression.

Quick-Start Guide

1. **Set the rules:** Introduce the challenge and explain that every sentence must both include a candy bar name and stay on topic with your unit of study. For example: "We have three types of bones in our hand: the carpals, the metacarpals, and the phalanges. Taken together, these items form the *3 Musketeers* of the hand bones!"
2. **Brainstorm candy bars:** Provide a massive list of candy names (e.g., Twix, Snickers, Milky Way) for students to use as inspiration.

(Pro tip: Want to generate a massive list of these items in a flash? AI is your friend!)

3. **Collaborate or compete:** Students can work individually, in pairs, or as teams to generate sentences. For a competitive twist, set a timer or establish timed rounds where students submit their most clever sentences. Task your learners with having everything ready to share with their classmates in a slideshow or on a printed sheet of paper when time expires.

4. **Reflect and revise:** Once the activity concludes, review the submissions as a class, highlighting the most creative and accurate responses.

Pedagogy Power-Up

Challenge students to compile their candy-themed sentences into a Google Slides presentation, devoting a single, eye-catching slide for each creation. Each slide can feature a sentence paired with an image, creative formatting, or even a candy-themed design. Share the presentations for peer review or display them and give your students the chance to play again and again after seeing the stellar submissions of their peers. You'll be amazed at how quickly the quality of your students' submissions will skyrocket across the board. A rising tide truly will lift all boats!

House Rules

- **AI idea bank:** Use AI tools like ChatGPT to brainstorm a word bank of candy names or generate sample sentences for students to critique, getting the creative juices flowing.
- **Slideshow share-out:** Have your students work in teams to showcase their share-outs using Google Slides presentations, making the final products even sweeter.
- **Timed rounds:** Create excitement with a competition format where teams brainstorm as many accurate, creative sentences as possible before time expires. Instead of announcing a winner based on sheer volume of replies, challenge your students to

select the very best of their team's creations and put them up against their peers.
- **Class gallery walk:** Print students' submissions and allow peers to review and vote on their favorites. Use rubrics or sticky notes for peer feedback. Then select a new prompt and play again!

Similar to knights receiving land, samurai received mounds of rice and grain on PayDay in exchange for their service.

UDL for the Win

This simple activity engages diverse learners through its emphasis on creativity, humor, and collaboration. Let's take a look at how it can bring forth a shining example of each UDL principle.

- **Engagement** (the w*hy* of learning): The Candy Bar Challenge adds an element of fun and humor to content-based learning, transforming a potentially routine task into a playful opportunity for students to express themselves. By encouraging students to incorporate candy names into content-driven sentences, the activity builds curiosity and motivation while making the learning process more memorable. Students can work individually or in groups, fostering choice and autonomy while creating an environment where laughter, creativity, and participation thrive.

- Example prompt: "The cell membrane protects the cell by allowing selective passage—think of it like the *Milky Way*, forming a galaxy of safety around everything inside!"
- For students who need additional scaffolding, you can set specific content prompts (e.g., "Explain the water cycle," "Describe a historical event") and provide a list of preapproved candy names to spark inspiration.

- **Representation** (the *what* of learning): This activity incorporates multiple means of representation, offering students accessible entry points to engage with the material. A brainstormed list of candy names—easily generated with tools like ChatGPT—gives students a starting point. Sample sentences can serve as models, and students can experiment with both written and visual formats. Whether digitally creating a presentation, designing candy-themed illustrations, or sharing sentences verbally, the activity ensures content is accessible for all types of learners.

Pro tip: For some visual panache, encourage students to incorporate candy logos, illustrations, or relevant design elements into the work products that they create. Then turn creation into presentation by encouraging students to read sentences aloud with dramatic flair during the class review.

- **Action and expression** (the *how* of learning): The Candy Bar Challenge provides flexible options for students to demonstrate their understanding. Learners can choose to write sentences, collaborate on group slideshows, or pair visuals with their candy-themed wordplay. By emphasizing both quantity (brainstorming multiple ideas) and quality (crafting polished, content-driven responses), the activity meets students where they are and challenges them to stretch their skills.

This activity is a perfect blend of academic rigor and playful pedagogy. Watch as student participation soars, creativity flows, and the quality of submissions rises with each round. After all, a little candy-inspired competition might just be the sweetest way to make learning stick.

THE AMAZIN' ONLINE MARKETPLACE

Game On
Students design a fictional product related to your unit of study and create their very own Amazon-style product pages right in Google Slides! Each team crafts a full product portfolio, featuring key sections like a product description, Q&A, related items, and customer reviews. This activity taps into real-world media literacy and content mastery, making learning fun, purposeful, and collaborative.

A Universal Upgrade
This playful Amazon-style format deepens content understanding, sparks creativity, and engages diverse learners through UDL principles—a huge improvement on generic presentations.

Quick-Start Guide

1. **Set the scene:** Take a screenshot of a bunch of actual Amazon product pages. Explain that students will recreate them, but instead of actual products, they'll have to invent imaginative items connected to your current lesson. For example:
   - A Revolutionary War unit might lead to a "Patriot Power Pack" (survival kit of must-have items for soldiers on the front lines).
   - A biology unit might lead to a "Cell Membrane Defender" (a forcefield gadget featuring a wish list of products that would be essential for any aspiring organelle).

2. **Design templates:** Open a blank Google Slide and paste your real Amazon screenshot right inside it using the template builder tool (that way, students won't accidentally delete this image or move it around the page). Then drop a few handy click-and-drag text boxes onto the image, placing them over fields like product title, description, reviews, and Q&A. This simple trick will give your students the chance to type right over the actual listing and match the format of the genuine article.
3. **Assign team roles:** Students will fill these roles within their groups as they collaborate:
    - Product designer: Writes the item's description and features.
    - Q&A specialist: Creates and answers sample customer questions.
    - Feedback strategist: Crafts creative, positive, or critical reviews.
    - Marketing lead: Develops related products and catchy visuals.
4. **Showcase and share:** Teams present their product pages in a class gallery walk or slideshow showcase. Peers can vote on most creative, funny, or informative designs.

Pedagogy Power-Up

This activity blends real-world media literacy with creative problem-solving as students analyze professional product pages and replicate their structure to apply content knowledge. By connecting unit concepts to imaginative products, students sharpen critical thinking while showcasing accuracy and creativity. Collaborative storytelling through role-sharing and peer feedback encourages teamwork, revision, and polished final designs that reflect deeper understanding.

House Rules

- **Tech tip:** Share tools like Remove.bg to help students create super clean product visuals with transparent backgrounds.

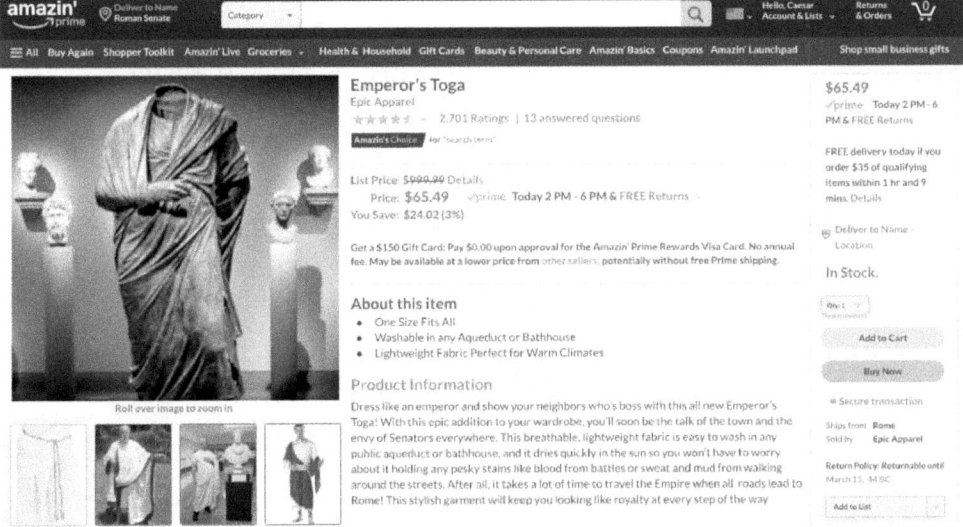

- **Timed competition:** Set rounds for specific tasks, or task each team with completing a certain number of slides, one at a time, alternating between creating and sharing as each round gets progressively more challenging and impressive.

UDL for the Win

This activity engages diverse learners through its emphasis on creativity, humor, and collaboration. With minimal advance teacher prep required, this sneaky approach to student-centered presentation shines across every facet of UDL.

- **Engagement** (the w*hy* of learning): Students take ownership of learning with a real-world, imaginative twist. Choice and collaboration empower them to showcase their understanding in ways that feel relevant and fun.
- **Representation** (the w*hat* of learning): The familiar Amazon format offers clear, structured fields (product title, Q&A, reviews) for students to organize ideas, blending text and visuals for accessibility.
- **Action and expression** (the *how* of learning): Students demonstrate knowledge creatively, whether through writing product

descriptions, designing visuals, or collaborating on Q&As. Flexible roles allow learners to lean into their strengths.

This activity transforms content review into an engaging, real-world challenge where imagination and learning collide. By connecting concepts to creative products, students gain a deeper understanding while flexing their media literacy skills in a format they see every day. Get ready to see some *Amazin'* results!

ALPHABLAST

Game On

In AlphaBLAST, student teams must "blast away" a board of letters—one at a time—by coming up with relevant, content-based words that start with each letter. Each word must connect to a "secret mission" (a unit-aligned topic), and students must be prepared to justify their choices if they're called into question. With layers of gameplay variety, this fast-paced activity fosters collaboration, quick thinking, and deep content connections.

A Universal Upgrade

Unlike traditional word-based review activities and "gotcha" tests, AlphaBLAST transforms classroom learning into a high-energy, team-driven showdown. By blending strategy, creativity, and on-the-fly thinking, this activity taps into the UDL principles.

Quick-Start Guide

1. **Set the scene:** In this head-to-head showdown, students are divided into teams of rival spacecraft that are navigating a dangerous meteor shower. Their task? Blast asteroids (letters) off the board by coming up with valid, content-relevant words related to the day's secret mission. For example, If the secret mission is the American Revolution, teams might choose letters like these:

- P (for Paul Revere)
- B (for Boston Tea Party)

2. Share the rules of play:
- The class starts with a board featuring a grid of twenty-six letters (like the one pictured nearby).
- Teams take turns choosing letters and providing a word with a quick justification for their selection.
- Invalid answers or delayed responses result in a hit to the team's "shields."

3. Consider gameplay variations:
- Hidden point values: Assign hidden scores to letters (e.g., vowels = 1 point, rare letters = 3 points). Reveal points as letters are blasted.
- Fixed points: Give each letter a visible score (like Scrabble) to guide team strategy.
- Column challenge: Start at the bottom of a letter column and work upward, earning points in *Space Invaders* style.
- Double letters: Place multiple instances of certain letters to allow broader word choices.
- Random symbols/numbers: Swap in symbols or numbers that students must creatively connect to the secret mission.

4. Work independently: Individual teams work to come up with as many unique answers as they can, then share their findings to cancel out duplicate responses that appear on more than one team's list (Scattergories style).

5. Reflect and revise: At the end of the game, review the words as a class. Discuss standout connections, justify tricky answers, and highlight teamwork wins.

Pedagogy Power-Up

AlphaBLAST combines quick, engaging gameplay with serious content mastery. Students must collaborate under pressure, connect ideas creatively, and articulate their reasoning—all while exploring content in fresh, memorable ways. Its flexible rules allow teachers to adapt the game for different learning goals, making it as simple or complex as needed.

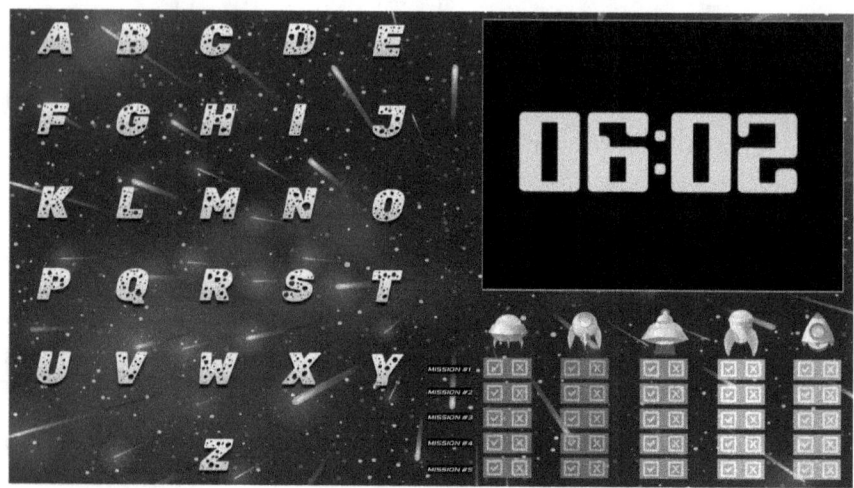

House Rules

- **Tech twist:** Use AI tools like ChatGPT to brainstorm possible secret missions or generate challenging prompts.
- **Class leaderboard:** Keep track of top-scoring teams to foster friendly competition across multiple rounds or days.
- **Timer tension:** Use dramatic countdown timers to add excitement and pace to the game.

UDL for the Win

AlphaBLAST takes the "Universal" part of UDL into a whole new dimension of fun for learners of any age. Using little more than a grid of twenty-six letters, you can get students' creative problem-solving engines firing on all cylinders in no time.

- **Engagement** (the *why* of learning): The competitive, high-energy format keeps students motivated and focused. Multiple gameplay options let you adapt the challenge to any classroom.

- **Representation** (the *what* of learning): Visual timers, flexible letter boards, and collaborative justification offer multiple pathways to access the game.
- **Action and expression** (the *how* of learning): Students think, speak, and strategize as they justify their word choices—providing verbal and content-based demonstrations of understanding.

This low-prep, high-engagement activity turns learning into an out-of-this-world experience where creativity and collaboration take center stage. With endless ways to mix things up, AlphaBLAST is a surefire way to energize your classroom.

QUESTIONS FOR DISCUSSION

1. The story of Lt. Gilbert Daniels highlighted the pitfalls of designing for the "average" and the transformative power of adaptable systems. Reflect on your teaching practices. Are there areas where you might still be unintentionally designing for an "average" student? How might you reimagine these areas to embrace individual variability and foster greater inclusivity?
2. UDL's principles emphasize meeting students where they are. Reflect on a recent lesson or unit. How did it support these principles? Are there opportunities to provide more flexible options for student participation, content delivery, or demonstrations of learning in future activities?
3. The critique of buzzer-style games like Kahoot! highlights the importance of inclusive design in classroom activities. Think about a competitive or game-based activity you use regularly. What modifications might you make to ensure all students, including those who process information differently or face unique challenges, can engage meaningfully and equitably?

YOU CAN'T USE UP CREATIVITY. THE MORE YOU USE, THE MORE YOU HAVE.

— MAYA ANGELOU

CHAPTER 2

SPARK THE SHIFT

CREATIVITY AND PLAYFUL INSPIRATION

The Mann Gulch fire roared like a living beast, a wall of flame racing through the steep Montana canyon on a dry August morning in 1949. The air trembled with heat and the crackle of burning trees, a symphony of destruction. At the edge stood fifteen brave young men. They weren't running from the fire—they had dived directly into it. Their heroic faces streaked with soot and determination, these smoke jumpers were young, strong, and trained for the job. But nothing could prepare them for what lay ahead.

The team had been called in to contain what seemed at first to be a manageable wildfire that was sparked by the previous night's lightning storm in the Helena National Forest. Their arrival by parachute, an almost routine operation for this elite crew, was immediately fraught with complications. Equipment was scattered across the rugged landscape, and their only radio—a lifeline to the outside world—was smashed on impact. They were alone.

Their leader, foreman Wagner Dodge, scanned the horizon with a practiced eye. He had seen plenty of fires before, but something about this one felt . . . wrong. The team made their way down into the gorge, but, by late afternoon, the inferno turned. A sudden gust of wind shifted its course, funneling flames up the canyon faster than anyone could have anticipated. The fire, now estimated to be advancing at thirty miles per hour, bore down on the men like a freight train. Thick smoke filled the air, choking out visibility. Dodge barked orders to his crew: "Drop your tools! Head for the ridge!" They abandoned their Pulaskis and shovels, sprinting up the steep incline in a desperate bid to outrun the searing flames that now climbed some thirty to fifty feet into the air.

But the ridge was far, the slope punishing, and the fire faster. Dodge could see the futility of their escape. Years of firefighting had honed his instincts, but this situation called for something more—a willingness to defy convention and think on his feet.

In a moment of clarity, Wagner Dodge stopped running and did the unthinkable.

Pulling a match from his pocket, he struck it against the rocky ground and set fire to the grass at his feet. The flames consumed the dry fuel quickly, leaving a blackened patch in their wake. It was an audacious, unheard-of maneuver: an escape fire, meant to rob the approaching blaze of anything left to burn.

"Come here! Get in the black!" Dodge shouted, his voice cutting through the chaos. But his men, untrained in the strategy and gripped by panic, were unable to follow his lead. As his fellow smoke jumpers kept running. Dodge wet a handkerchief, pressed it to his face, and lay down in the burned-out circle, clutching the earth as the firestorm surged over him.

When the flames passed, Dodge stood alone in his charred sanctuary. Around him, the gulch was a hellscape of ash and twisted metal. Tragically, thirteen of his men lost their lives that day, overcome by the fire they couldn't escape. Only two others, Robert Sallee and Walter Rumsey, had managed to reach a rocky outcrop where the flames couldn't reach.

The Mann Gulch fire was one of the deadliest tragedies in wildland firefighting history, claiming thirteen lives in a single, brutal afternoon.[14] Yet out of its ashes came a transformative lesson: Creativity can mean the difference between life and death. Wagner Dodge's escape fire, born of sheer necessity and a spark of ingenuity, saved his life and redefined firefighting strategy as we know it. His actions remind us that true innovation often arises in the face of chaos, when we are "really bothered" by something important and real. And seventy years later, the Mann Gulch fire endures as a symbol of resilience and adaptation. Dodge's legacy inspires us to think boldly, act decisively, and find clarity even in the most overwhelming of flames.

Revolutionary opportunities often begin in the fires of discomfort. Like Dodge, teachers don't have time to sit idly, waiting for help to arrive. The world is changing too fast, and passive learning isn't preparing our students for it. If we want them to be problem solvers, we must light our own escape fires—breaking free from passive instruction and embracing creativity as a survival skill.

Creativity, in this context, isn't just about making fancy art projects or designing elaborate bulletin boards. It's the ability to think flexibly, solve problems under pressure, and adapt to unexpected challenges. It's a skill, not a talent—and like any skill, it can be taught, nurtured, and modeled. Whether you're dodging wildfires or leading a classroom,

---

14 Norman Maclean, *Young Men and Fire: A True Story of the Mann Gulch Fire* (University of Chicago Press, 1992).

creativity is the spark that turns uncertainty into opportunity. It's not just an advantage; it's essential.

Resilience and innovation emerge in the face of adversity, of unprecedented challenges. And in the classroom, this mindset of resourceful creativity and nimble problem-solving is what separates passive learning from true engagement.

FROM BURNING BRIGHT TO SHINING ON

Wagner Dodge's quick thinking reminds us that moments of crisis demand both courage and innovation. Decades later, educators around the world found themselves in a similarly uncharted inferno—this time, in the form of a global pandemic.

When COVID-19 shuttered schools in March 2020, educators had to think fast. Much like Wagner Dodge's ingenuity reshaped firefighting, the pandemic forced teachers, administrators, and staff to rewrite the playbook for education in the thick of chaos. They became unsung heroes, responding with resourcefulness and innovation that redefined what schools could be.

Administrators transformed school cafeterias into food banks, stepping up to support families suddenly juggling childcare and work. School counselors held virtual office hours late into the night, offering lifelines to students in need. IT specialists worked with tech companies to secure software licenses and hardware for families without reliable internet. And teachers, armed with little more than their wits and willpower, found ways to make learning happen—hosting Zoom lessons with shower walls turned into whiteboards, fashioning new tools from whatever they had on hand. Everywhere you looked, we adapted, innovated, and showed the world that learning could happen anywhere. Because it had to.

These weren't just temporary fixes; they were testaments to the resilience and boundless creativity of the teaching profession. Even as schools reopened and routines returned, many of these innovations stuck—a reminder that disruption often brings opportunity.

Some of the most effective pandemic-era changes, like flexible scheduling, digital collaboration tools, online parent-teacher conferences, and student-centered instructional models, aren't just lingering; they're becoming standard practice. And, you know what? Now that you mention it, a lot of those little conveniences we first adopted out of necessity (like Uber Eats dropping food at our doorstep or restaurant menus that magically appear with a quick QR code scan) aren't just sticking around—they're making life easier across the board.

Many schools that once resisted tech integration are now embracing hybrid and flipped learning models. Snowstorms used to mean a full week off. Now, virtual learning can keep students on track (well, more or less). And those rigid late-work policies? Teachers have begun rethinking their stance, drawing from their own experiences during pandemic upheaval to infuse more grace and empathy into their classrooms. At the core of all this change is a powerful reminder that the brain itself is more adaptable than we ever imagined.

Which brings us to the work of Marian Diamond.

DIAMONDS ARE FOREVER

Marian Diamond, celebrated as a pioneer of modern neuroscience, made history by proving that the brain is not a static organ but one that can adapt and grow through enriched experiences. Her groundbreaking research ultimately culminated in her chance to map millions of tiny neural pathways in the brain of none other than our old friend Albert Einstein, uncovering fascinating insights into the field of science that we now call neuroplasticity. This work laid the foundation for understanding how our environment and experiences can profoundly shape our cognitive abilities, revolutionizing the fields of education and child development.

But like any self-respecting woman of science, Dr. Diamond didn't start out by testing her theories on human beings (even if their organs had been posthumously donated to the cause). As it turns out, the structure and function of the human brain is remarkably similar to that of a lab rat. So that's exactly where she began her work.

Throughout the 1960s, Diamond conducted a series of experiments that showed how enriched environments could physically change the brains of lab rats. She placed one group of rats in a stimulating setting with toys, tunnels, and other rats to interact with, while another group lived in isolated, barren cages. Over time, the rats in the enriched environments developed thicker cerebral cortices—parts of the brain responsible for thinking and memory. This growth was attributed to myelination, a sort of mental paving process that strengthens connections between neural pathways across what's known as the brain's glial cells.

But the brains of those rats who were excluded from all the fun? Not so much.

Like a muscle, the brain grows stronger with use. Diamond's findings revolutionized our understanding of brain plasticity, proving that neurons that fire together wire together. This work laid the foundation for modern education and child development, reminding us that when it comes to the brain, if you don't use it, you lose it. Naturally, this leads us to consider a ton of practical implications as we blaze new pathways and design lesson plans for ingenious young minds at work (and at play).

Marian Diamond's work on enriched environments underscores the profound and lasting impact of active engagement on cognitive development. Recent studies on cognitive endurance build on Diamond's findings, showing that purposeful engagement not only improves immediate performance but also fosters long-term resilience. Active learning strategies—storytelling, model building, even AI-powered simulations—ignite curiosity and growth in ways that are both authentic and accessible. Yet access to these strategies is not evenly distributed. Research shows that students from disadvantaged backgrounds often face steeper declines in performance over time, highlighting the urgent need for equitable access to enriching educational experiences.

A 2022 working paper from the National Bureau of Economic Research highlights this disparity, showing that active engagement reduces cognitive fatigue errors by 22 percent and enhances performance across tasks for up to five months. However, the research also reveals a troubling gap: Black and Hispanic students experience cognitive performance declines 72 percent faster than their peers, underscoring the need for equitable access to active learning opportunities across the board.

The findings are clear. Active learning works, but only if it is sustained and accessible for all students.

We often hear talk about the achievement gap. But studies like this one are proof positive that the *opportunity gap* is every bit as vital. We must create environments where all students can thrive, regardless of their starting point.

Which, of course, brings us back to the power of UDL—a framework that places creativity, flexibility, and student empowerment at the center of the learning experience.

In our classrooms, enrichment can take many forms. Picture students engaged in project-based learning with collaborative groups, manipulatives, or immersive experiences like field trips (even if they're powered by AI). Imagine spaces where creativity flows through activities like sketchnoting, LEGO building, or Play-Doh modeling—giving students the tools to explore abstract concepts in hands-on, tangible ways. Enrichment doesn't have to mean expensive technology or elaborate setups; it can be as simple as fostering curiosity through meaningful challenges, peer collaboration, and choice-driven tasks.

When students engage in meaningful challenges—solving complex problems or participating in interactive activities—their brains adapt, grow, and build endurance. This endurance isn't just about surviving the rigors of education; it's about thriving, finding clarity, and developing the resilience to face life's challenges. It's the same kind of resilience we see modeled in Dodge's escape fire, where adaptation and innovation proved to be lifesaving.

The illusion of learning, on the other hand, is the false confidence students feel when passively absorbing information while listening to lectures, skimming textbooks, or completing rote tasks. It mistakes time spent sitting in a seat for time spent actively engaging the brain's glial cells and strengthening the connections that drive deeper understanding. The results? Far from enriched or encouraging.

Harvard professor Louis Deslauriers's research highlights this critical gap. While students may gravitate toward lectures for their simplicity, they consistently outperform their peers when engaged in active learning strategies. Hands-on experiments, collaborative problem-solving, and dynamic discussions force students to apply their knowledge in real time, transforming abstract concepts into actionable insights. This is process is more demanding, but it fosters deeper understanding, longer retention, and a stronger bridge between knowing and doing.

As Dr. Deslauriers succinctly puts it: "Study after study shows that student evaluations seem to be completely uncorrelated with actual learning. . . . A superstar lecturer can explain things in such a way as to make students feel like they are learning more than they actually are [but] deep learning is hard work."[15]

Addressing the illusion of learning versus actual learning likely does not involve a return to the comfort of lecture-heavy instruction. Instead, the escape fire we need might be smoldering in the form of active, enriched learning strategies. It's time to embrace the challenge, let go of outdated habits, and lose the lecture for good—even if it feels counterintuitive to do so.

The best part? UDL reminds us that designing for the margins can light a fire of creativity that benefits everyone. By thoughtfully incorporating creative sparks—like hands-on projects, dynamic simulations, or personalized feedback systems—teachers can reignite excitement and

---

15 Peter Reuell, "Lessons in Learning," Harvard Gazette, September 4, 2019, https://news.harvard.edu/gazette/story/2019/09/study-shows-that-students-learn-more-when-taking-part-in-classrooms-that-employ-active-learning-strategies/.

breathe new life into their classrooms, turning ordinary moments into extraordinary opportunities for growth, connection, and discovery.

Industry experts even have a term for this: *the happiness advantage.*

A CHEAT CODE TO PLAY BETTER

Marian Diamond's research shows that enriched environments strengthen the brain. But what if we could supercharge those environments even further? According to Harvard researcher Shawn Achor, joy itself can act like a cognitive escape fire, rewiring the brain to become more resilient, focused, and creative.

Achor's work, popularized in *The Happiness Advantage*, reveals that when students experience positive emotions, their brains release dopamine and serotonin—chemicals that boost learning, memory, and problem-solving. In other words, happy brains work better.

This isn't just feel-good fluff. Achor's research shows that happiness can make people up to 300 percent more creative and productive. In the classroom, that translates to students who take more intellectual risks, persist longer through challenges, and engage more deeply with content.[16]

For teachers, the implications are staggering.

Like Dodge's escape fire, joy creates space. It lowers cognitive load, opens new paths, and helps students push through the tough stuff with confidence and curiosity. Whether through playful games, hands-on projects, or tech-powered exploration, sparking joy in the classroom fuels more than just smiles. It lights the fire for serious academic growth.

And when that spark becomes part of the daily routine? That's the cheat code. A classroom built on creativity and joy isn't just more fun; it's more effective.

So let's move from theory to action and explore how some creative sparks can light a fire for learning in your classroom. Here are five playful

---

16 Shawn Achor, *The Happiness Advantage* (Crown Publishing Group, 2018).

ways to ignite your students with immediate creative energy. Whether you're leveraging technology or reimagining your classroom space, each of these strategies works for learners of any age, in any content area, and at any stage of your lesson flow—from warm-ups and brain breaks to formative assessments and beyond.

START WITH A STORY

Stories have an unparalleled ability to ignite our imagination and spark creativity. The best movie trailers open with "In a world where . . ." and invite us to step into new realms, connect seemingly unrelated ideas, and dream bigger than before. A single suggestion can send our minds racing to unlock endless possibilities. In the classroom, storytelling becomes a gateway to exploration, allowing students to weave their learning into something dynamic and meaningful.

If you're looking to shake up creativity in your next lesson plan, Rory's Story Cubes are ready to roll.

These chunky, dice-like cubes feature simple, evocative images (a magnifying glass, a lightning bolt, a set of footprints), and the challenge for your students is to connect these symbols to whatever they're learning in class. How might the magnifying glass symbolize the scientific method? Could a lightning bolt represent a breakthrough discovery or an important moment in history? If so, what discovery might that be? With over ten million possible combinations from a standard nine-cube set, no two rolls are likely to result in the same story. This activity pushes students to think critically and creatively as they bridge the gap between abstract course content and tangible, visual cues.

Now for the fun twist: The cubes come in a wide variety of themed sets that probably have nothing to do with what you're studying—think Batman, Harry Potter, Scooby-Doo, and more. And that's precisely the point. These quirky, off-the-wall images force students to make lateral connections between a universe they already understand and the material you're teaching. Maybe the Bat-Signal becomes a metaphor for ethical decision-making in a college-level philosophy class, or Scooby-Doo's famous sandwich inspires a seventh-grade biology student to explain keystone species and the *food* chain (get it?). The more unexpected the connections, the more creative and meaningful the learning becomes.

To increase engagement, keep a handful of these themed cube sets on hand, and let students or teams choose their preferred collection. Or, for another fun twist, give teams the power to assign themed sets to rival teams and watch them adapt to whatever curveballs come their way. Each group then crafts a story that weaves their images into your lesson content, using collaboration and quick thinking to create connections that are as creative as they are informative. By embracing the oddball nature of the dice, students are encouraged to think critically, synthesize knowledge, and create stories with lasting impact.

For a digital variation, platforms like the Noun Project offer millions of free icons that can serve as the foundation for similar activities.

There's even a free Google Slides extension that allows you to search and drag icons directly into your presentation slides, clip-art style. Teachers can provide students with random collections of quirky icons and challenge them to craft narratives that connect each image to class content. The flexibility of digital tools allows for customization while keeping the focus on creativity and connection.

To take this activity further, try adding collaborative or competitive elements. Teams can work together to build a single story, present their narratives to the class, or compete with their classmates to see which squad can dream up the most (or the most innovative) connections. Award bonus points for creativity, thematic coherence, or cleverness in tying content to their dice rolls. Wrap up with reflection questions: How did they generate their connections? What strategies helped their team succeed? How did the unexpected pairings deepen their understanding of the material?

Whether your class is rolling physical cubes or curating digital icons, this activity transforms learning into a playful, imaginative exercise. Students aren't just recalling facts—they're discovering connections, sharing perspectives, and making meaning in ways that are uniquely their own.

GET DRAWN TOGETHER

It's true, what they say: A picture really is worth a thousand words. Art has a unique ability to spark creativity, distill complex ideas, and make abstract concepts tangible. Like the most mesmerizing illustrations in a favorite book or the vivid panels of a graphic novel, visuals invite us to see the world through a new lens. A single sketch can connect seemingly unrelated ideas, ignite curiosity, and inspire deeper understanding.

In the classroom, drawing becomes more than just an artistic exercise—it's a bridge between thinking and doing. It transforms learning into a hands-on, visual exploration that engages students in powerful ways. And if you're feeling extra creative, try blending traditional techniques like sketchnoting with cutting-edge, AI-powered tools.

Here's an example. Instead of writing paragraphs about yesterday's lesson, why not encourage your students to draw what they know? Sketchnoting combines doodling, labels, and annotations to visually

capture ideas. Make no mistake: This isn't about artistic ability! Stick figures are more than welcome; arrows, shapes, and abstract squiggles are even better. The goal isn't perfection but thoughtful engagement with the material. As students translate their understanding into images, they naturally slow down and think deeply about the concepts they're putting on the page.

The magic of sketchnoting lies in its accessibility. Students can annotate their sketches, explaining the details and connections behind each element. This approach strengthens their comprehension while creating a unique, personal representation of the material that is so satisfyingly Socratic ("Why did you say what you said?"). Sketchnoting is a game changer for students of all ages, offering a creative outlet that transforms abstract ideas into concrete visual depictions that stick.

For a tech-savvy twist, the teacher can even helm an AI art-generation tool while students collaborate to craft descriptive prompts. As students refine their language to generate specific imagery—whether it's a visual representation of a historical event, a scientific concept, or a literary theme—they sharpen their critical thinking and communication skills. Teams or individuals can compete to provide the most vivid, relevant descriptions and see how closely the generated image matches their expectations. The process is collaborative, fun, and packed with opportunities for growth.

Want to flip the script? Present students with an AI-generated image and challenge them to reverse engineer the secret recipe you used to create the artistic masterpiece before them. How much can they write about what they see in the image? What are the key details, textures, and colors? Encourage students to think critically about every element of the visual and describe it as vividly as possible.

Once they've crafted their descriptions, feed their write-ups back into the AI tool to generate a new image. Then, compare the results with the original. How close did they come? This playful exercise transforms close reading and precise writing into an exciting challenge, where even stick-figure observations can spark lively discussions. It's a devilishly fun way to reinforce the importance of detail, descriptive accuracy, and the creative process.

Whether students are sketching by hand or crafting collaborative prompts, it's important to keep in mind that the focus isn't ever about creating the perfect work of art—it's on the journey of discovery, creativity, and connection. Visual creativity empowers students to think critically, engage deeply, and express their ideas in ways that go beyond words. With tools like sketchnoting and teacher-guided AI artwork, learning becomes a canvas for curiosity, where every line, squiggle, and description brings new possibilities to life.

"GEORGE WASHINGTON"

For this mash-up, we combined the WOOD emoji with the smiling face full of TEETH. Legend says that George Washington had wooden teeth (but they weren't actually made of wood).

This emoji is a mix of the FIREWORKS emoji and the MILITARY MEDAL. Washington was a famous general in the American Revolution, and he won our independence on July 4.

Washington is part GOAT and part KING. The Goat stands for "Greatest of All Time" because he was the first President of the USA. He's also like a King because he had the chance to be the king of the USA.

MASH UP TWO EXISTING IDEAS

If you're ever stuck for a creative kick-start, remember that what's old can become new again (and again, and again!). Mash-ups—those delightful combinations of two familiar ideas into something entirely fresh—ignite creativity, challenging us to see connections we might have otherwise overlooked. Think of your favorite songs that borrow riffs from iconic hits or those hilarious memes that blend pop culture references into one unforgettable punchline. In the classroom, mash-ups become a playful way for students to reimagine what they're learning, blending symbols, concepts, or even characters into something uniquely their own.

And what better way to explore this than with everyone's favorite universal language: emoji.

Using free online tools like Emoji Kitchen (just a quick Google search away) or the Genmoji tools that are built right into iOS devices, students can create custom emoji hybrids that bring their learning to life. Imagine asking your class to use brand-new emoji mash-ups to convey the most important themes of *Romeo and Juliet*. Suddenly, you've got eager squads of students remixing their favorite icons into clever combinations like a cross between the infamous broken red heart emoji and the haunting skull face emoji. What story does this combination tell? How does it reflect the tragedy of Shakespeare's star-crossed lovers? Students can experiment endlessly with mash-ups like these, generating creative combinations that represent key ideas, characters, or themes from your lessons.

Once students create their custom emojis, take the activity a step further by having them explain their choices: Why did they select these particular symbols? What connections do they see between their mash-up and the material covered in class? This reflective step encourages critical thinking and pushes students to articulate their understanding in fresh, innovative ways. You could also challenge students to invite their classmates to interpret the deeper symbolism behind each mash-up. This playful approach fosters collaboration and sparks engaging discussions as students explore how their peers tackled the same challenge.

Prefer a tech-free approach? No sweat. Take the same activity offline with nothing more than a few markers or colored pencils and some blank paper. Students can draw their emoji creations, adding personal flair to each design. Encourage them to pair their drawings with explanations that unpack their choices and reasoning. This is about connecting ideas, explaining choices, and engaging with content in meaningful ways. Whether students are working with digital tools or markers and paper, you're inspiring them to explore, invent, and express their understanding in creative new ways, turning abstract ideas into tangible, visual representations.

Now you're cookin'!

CONSTRUCT A MONUMENT TO UNDERSTANDING

There's something universally satisfying about building things with our hands. As kids, we stack blocks; as adults, we assemble trendy IKEA furniture (or try to). Creating something physical brings ideas to life in ways that words alone can't. Building isn't just about the final product—it's about the process of testing, refining, and reimagining until everything clicks into place.

In the classroom, building becomes a hands-on way for students to make sense of abstract ideas. Whether it's snapping together LEGO bricks or designing digital worlds, these activities encourage critical thinking, collaboration, and innovation. We remember that sometimes the best way to learn is to build.

Few tools are as timeless and versatile as those aforementioned LEGO bricks. Practically indestructible (just watch your step!), these colorful blocks are a surefire hit for students of all ages. Simply drop a bag or bucket onto a desk and challenge your students to create 3D representations of key concepts or content from your current unit. The possibilities are endless: Build historical landmarks to represent pivotal moments in history, model scientific processes like the water cycle, or design abstract representations of literary themes. LEGO's simplicity means the focus isn't on intricate designs but on the reasoning behind them.

Each build becomes an opportunity for reflection. Ask students to explain their choices: Why did they use that piece? How does the structure reflect what they've learned? By articulating their thinking, students deepen their understanding of the content while strengthening metacognitive skills. With LEGO, the journey is just as valuable as the finished product. Trial and error pushes students to think critically, solve problems, and make abstract ideas tangible—all while building something they can be proud of.

Take the activity further by incorporating a tech twist. Once students complete their builds, have them snap photos of their creations and upload them to a shared Google Slides presentation (or similar collaborative platform). On each slide, students can annotate their designs with captions explaining how their creations connect to the material. Then comes the real fun: Tear those bad boys apart and build something entirely new. Using the same finite set of supplies, students can create multiple representations of their learning, refining their ideas with every iteration.

This cycle of building, documenting, and reflecting transforms a hands-on activity into a powerful exercise in creativity, collaboration, and critical thinking. It challenges students to push beyond surface-level engagement and approach their learning with curiosity and adaptability. Building isn't just about constructing physical objects—it's about constructing understanding. By pairing tactile learning with thoughtful reflection, students gain the tools to build ideas that stick around long after the blocks come down.

> **Pro tip:** See that eye-popping photo of an epic speech being delivered in front of the Reflecting Pool on the National Mall in Washington, DC? That's actually a fusion of real LEGO bricks and a digital backdrop. All you need to do is use an AI image generator or library to find or create a picture, place your physical LEGO construction right in front of your laptop screen, and snap a photo!

GET MESSY WITH 3D MODELS

Roll up your sleeves! Learning takes on a whole new dimension when students shape ideas into something they see or even hold. Whether they're molding concepts with Play-Doh or crafting intricate worlds in Minecraft, students will use these hands-on activities to turn abstract ideas into interactive, concrete creations. The process isn't just about what they build but about how they build it: trial, error, and discovering how elements fit together to tell a story or solve a problem.

The act of building immerses students in their learning. It engages their spatial reasoning, critical thinking, and creativity in ways no lecture ever could. Ready to dive in? Here's how to spark curiosity and challenge perspectives by being just a little bit messier—in the best possible way.

Few tools are as simple yet versatile as Play-Doh. Hand out mini tubs of this squishy, colorful modeling clay and challenge students to sculpt models that represent key concepts from your current unit. Perhaps middle schoolers use Play-Doh to form visualizations of the water cycle, or high schoolers craft 3D representations of molecular structures. The pliable and often frustratingly fragile nature of Play-Doh encourages trial and error, teaching students to think critically about structure, stability, and design.

What makes Play-Doh so effective is its flexibility. Students can easily modify their creations as they work, blending creativity with problem-solving. The tactile nature of this activity allows learners of all ages to engage deeply with abstract ideas while having a little fun (and maybe getting a little messy). As students build and refine their models, they aren't just representing knowledge—they're constructing understanding.

For a digital twist, take the creativity online with Minecraft Education, a virtual sandbox where students can design anything from historical landmarks to geometric models. With endless possibilities at their fingertips, students can create 3D worlds that reflect the concepts they're exploring in class. Picture a history lesson where students reconstruct ancient civilizations brick by brick or a science class where they design ecosystems that thrive (or collapse) based on their choices.

But Minecraft isn't just about building; it's about sharing. Encourage students to create short video tutorials narrating their creative process. Channeling their favorite Twitch streamers or YouTube creators, students can explain the connections between their designs and your lesson's content. These presentations not only showcase their creations but also hone their communication and critical thinking skills.

Prefer to stay offline? Take the same principles of Minecraft Education and apply them to Play-Doh by challenging students to document their builds. Snap photos of their creations and upload them to a collaborative Google Slides deck where they can annotate their designs with explanations. Then, it's time to tear those suckers apart and start over, reimagining new ways to represent the content using the same materials.

Whether students are squishing clay or stacking virtual bricks, the goal remains the same: to create, refine, and connect. Remember that building isn't just about constructing physical models. It's about constructing understanding. And when students bring ideas to life, they don't just learn—they make their learning unforgettable.

A PLAYBOOK FOR CREATIVITY

For this chapter's playbook, we're shining a spotlight on a handful of the activities we've developed together since the publication of *Fully Engaged*. These take a bit more setup than the strategies we provided earlier in this chapter, but we've found them to be well worth the investment. Don't be afraid to use these as inspiration to light some creative fires of your own!

COINS FOR CONTENT

Game On
Turn your classroom into a dynamic financial challenge! In Coins for Content, students work within a set "budget" to create answers that maximize their learning. Inspired by real-world decision-making, this activity challenges students to prioritize valuable information and make thoughtful trade-offs, all while staying under budget.

A Creative Upgrade
This enhances standard classroom discussions by making budgeting a creative critical thinking challenge to maximize the value of reflection right down to the very last cent.

Quick-Start Guide

1. **Set the stage:** Create a target question or prompt tied to your unit of study. For example, "Explain the key causes of the American Revolution." Assign a coin value to different types of words:
    - High-value content words (e.g., specific historical terms) cost more.
    - Common or filler words (e.g., articles or conjunctions) cost less.
2. **Create a budget:** Give each student or team a set budget (e.g., $1.35) and distribute coins (real, printed, or virtual) to represent their funds.
3. **Shop for words:** Students draft their responses by "purchasing" additional words that only their team can use. They must stay within their budget while ensuring their answer is as complete and detailed as possible.
4. **Present and reflect:** Students share their responses and explain their budgeting choices. Encourage reflection on why they spent more on certain words and how they balanced their priorities.

Pedagogy Power-Up

Introduce a competitive element by awarding bonus coins to teams that include specifically selected high-value, targeted content words from your lessons or unit. For example, using critical terms like *lysosome* or *Golgi apparatus* in a biology unit earns additional points. This adds an extra incentive for deeper critical thinking and careful planning.

House Rules

Leverage tools like ChatGPT to generate lists of specially selected high-value content words for your lesson. For example, ask your AI assistant, "What key vocabulary should students focus on when discussing photosynthesis?" AI tools can also provide sample responses to compare with student answers, encouraging analysis and improvement.

UDL for the Win

This activity seamlessly integrates UDL principles, turning a simple budgeting challenge into a dynamic learning experience across the board.

- **Engagement** (the *why* of learning): The budgeting element and team-based collaboration keep students motivated and invested. The competitive aspect adds excitement, while the reflection on spending choices fosters curiosity and critical thinking.
- **Representation** (the *what* of learning): The coin-based structure provides a concrete, visual representation of abstract decision-making, making the task accessible to all learners. Adjusting coin values or providing scaffolds ensures inclusivity across skill levels.
- **Action and expression** (the *how* of learning): Students can draft, revise, and present their responses in ways that match their strengths—verbally, through written responses, or

collaboratively as a team. The flexibility of this activity encourages creative problem-solving and diverse participation.

SWATCH WHAT HAPPENS

Game On
In Swatch What Happens, students reimagine your course content as a themed line of colored items like nail polishes, crayons, paint samples, or fabric swatches. Each shade must have a clever name tied to the subject matter and include a rationale that explains its connection. This activity encourages all kinds of creativity, deepens content understanding, and adds a colorful twist to any unit!

A Creative Upgrade
This activity improves traditional content reviews as students blend artistry and analysis to create vibrant connections to your curriculum!

Quick-Start Guide

1. **Set the theme:** Choose a topic related to your current unit (e.g., the Julius Caesar Crayon Collection for a Shakespeare unit or the Periodic Palette for chemistry).
2. **Swatch it out:** Provide students with inspiration like paint samples, fabric swatches, or digital tools for color creation. Students must develop at least three to five color names with clever connections to the topic and pair them with an explanation. For example:
   - Soothsayer Blues: Inspired by Artemidorus' ignored warning to Caesar, this deep blue reflects the sadness of unheeded advice.
   - Backstabber 23: A vivid crimson symbolizing betrayal, named after the infamous murder of Julius Caesar by Brutus and the senators.

3. **Incorporate a tactile element:** Visit your local hardware or craft store to grab free paint chips, fabric swatches, or color cards. Alternatively, let students use the web to find just the right shades.
4. **Share and showcase:** Students can present their collections to the class, explaining their rationale for each choice. For an added layer of fun, display their creations on a gallery wall or in a shared digital folder.

Pedagogy Power-Up

This game's got the best of both worlds: Students of all ages really love sorting through big old boxes of manipulatives, and retailers are more than happy to provide you with *tons* of these colorful samples for free if you just ask them! When you're done playing—er, learning—throw these items back into a resealable plastic tote and you're ready to add some color to whatever content comes your way.

House Rules

Invite students to use an AI-powered color identification tool or generator to create custom shades and hex codes that perfectly match their vision. For example, "What shade would best represent the Battle of Thermopylae?" AI can help refine their palettes and add a professional touch to their creations.

UDL for the Win

Swatch What Happens brilliantly blends creativity and content understanding with UDL principles, ensuring every learner can find their niche as they connect with content in ways that are as colorful as they are meaningful.

- **Engagement** (the *why* of learning): The colorful, hands-on nature of the activity keeps students excited and curious. Their personal connections to their swatches spark motivation, while the collaborative aspects encourage camaraderie and creativity.
- **Representation** (the *what* of learning): Using real-world materials like paint chips or digital tools provides multiple ways for students to access and connect with the content. Clear themes and examples make the task approachable for all learners, regardless of their starting point.
- **Action and expression** (the *how* of learning): Students express their understanding through artistic design, verbal rationale, and thematic storytelling. The flexibility to create both visually and conceptually allows every student to showcase their unique perspective.

CAVEMAN GRAMMAR

Game On

Travel back to the Stone Age and spark the fires of curiosity with Caveman Grammar! Inspired by the game Poetry for Neanderthals, this no-prep activity challenges students to explain complex concepts using only single-syllable words. It's the perfect blend of simplicity and strategy and will light up your classroom with laughter and learning.

A Creative Upgrade

Enhance traditional vocabulary reviews by having students grunt their way to mastery with single-syllable cues. Creativity gets primitive!

Quick-Start Guide

1. **Prepare the cards:** Provide each team with blank cards (index cards or digital slides) to create their own Caveman Grammar cards. Each card has two parts:
   - A basic term (e.g., *DNA*)
   - A more challenging word or phrase related to the basic term (e.g., *deoxyribonucleic acid*) that adds depth and difficulty

2. **Split into teams:** Divide the class into two teams. Each team creates a set of cards for their opponents to guess. Cards should align with your current unit of study.
3. **Set the rules:** When it's time to play, one student from each team becomes the caveman speaker. Their job is to shout out a string of single-syllable clues to help their teammates guess the basic term on the card. For example:
   - Speaker: "Small bits of stuff that make you, you!"
   - Teammates: "Ooh! That's DNA."
   - If their team guesses correctly, they can even push their luck and attempt the challenge phrase for bonus points!
4. **Time it:** Use a timer (e.g., sixty seconds) for each round.
5. **Score it:** Teams score points for each correct guess but lose points if the caveman speaker uses multisyllable words.

Pedagogy Power-Up

Encourage teams to create as many vocab cards as they can, then swap cards with opposing teams. (Or, to really up the stakes, collect a massive stack of cards in a single pile at the front of the classroom for every team to draw from.) For an added layer of hilarity, use a drumroll sound effect or flashing visuals when teams attempt to guess a bonus phrase.

House Rules

Skip the setup process and use AI tools like ChatGPT to generate a massive themed word list that will help get your classes in the game that much faster. Print the list out, cut it into strips, and your students are ready to play.

UDL for the Win

This activity hits the UDL trifecta in the most delightfully silly way! Talk about engagement—who doesn't love the hilarity of grunting their way through class content? This unconventional approach to vocabulary review hits all the right UDL notes.

- **Engagement** (the *why* of learning): The playful, game-based format keeps students laughing and fully immersed in the learning process. The friendly competition ensures high energy, while the novelty of the caveman theme sparks curiosity and excitement.
- **Representation** (the *what* of learning): Breaking down complex terms into single-syllable clues simplifies abstract ideas, making them accessible to all learners. Providing modeled examples or scaffolds ensures that students at varying levels can participate meaningfully.
- **Action and expression** (the *how* of learning): Students can create, interpret, and deliver clues, giving them multiple ways to demonstrate understanding. The scalable difficulty allows for differentiation, ensuring both struggling learners and advanced students are challenged and supported.

QUESTIONS FOR DISCUSSION

1. Marian Diamond's research on enriched environments highlights the transformative power of small changes in fostering growth. In your classroom, what barriers might exist to creating such an environment, and how can you creatively overcome them using the resources you already have?
2. Shawn Achor's *The Happiness Advantage* suggests that cultivating positivity can drive success. What steps can you take to integrate moments of joy and reflection into your daily routine? How might tools like gratitude journals or gamified recognition systems help make these practices sustainable?
3. This chapter introduced the concept of active learning as a way to combat the illusion of learning. Reflect on your current teaching practices. Where might you be unintentionally prioritizing coverage over connection? How can you shift your approach to make active discovery a more central part of your classroom experience?

AS MACHINES GET BETTER AT BEING MACHINES, HUMANS HAVE TO GET BETTER AT BEING MORE HUMAN.

— ANDREW J. SCOTT —

CHAPTER 3

TEACH WITH HEART

CONNECTION IN A TECH-DRIVEN WORLD

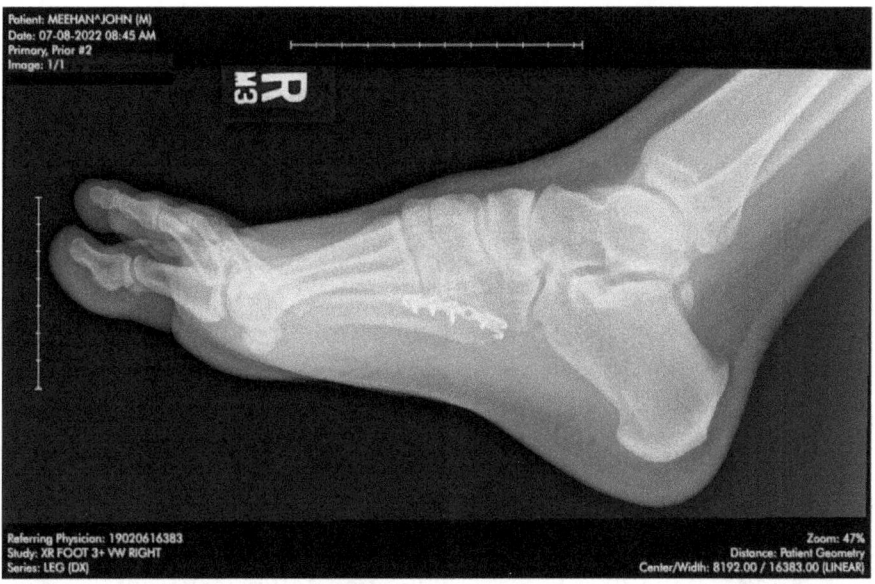

Hey, folks. John here. And this is the story of what technology sometimes forgets

It was the summer of 2022, and I found myself lying on a hospital bed in Northern Virginia, groggy from anesthesia and trying to shake off the cobwebs. Somewhere inside a securely encrypted app—accessible only after completing a two-factor authentication process—was the official report detailing my injury: "Examination of the right foot reveals swelling, ecchymosis, limited ROM of the ankle, and displaced tuberosity fracture of the fifth metatarsal."

In layman's terms, I broke my foot. And it hurt like hell.

As I read that sterile, clinical report, I couldn't shake the feeling that something was missing. The pain in my foot was real, but where in all this tech-powered super science was the acknowledgment of *me*—the person experiencing it?

Machines excel at solving problems and organizing massive amounts of data, but they often lack the warmth and nuance to recognize the humanity behind the numbers. That detachment, glaring in my medical report, left me wondering where the "human" fits in an increasingly machine-driven equation. Paradoxically, the more detailed the app's insights, the more alone I felt reading them.

At that moment, I realized something profound: Technology may make processes faster, but without human connection, it can feel pretty darn isolating—even dehumanizing. And if that's true in medicine, what does it mean for education, where meaningful human connections are the very foundation of learning?

This question of balancing precision and empathy extends far beyond the hospital bed. It reaches into education, creativity, and society at large, forcing us to consider how we ensure that human connection isn't lost amid technological efficiency.

At the very least, it's certainly a thought experiment worth further consideration.

And so, at the 2023 Future of Education Technology Conference in New Orleans, Louisiana, a keynote presenter decided to ask an audience just shy of ten thousand teachers from around the world to answer a question along the very same lines.

That speaker's name is Daniel Burrus, and he's a noted American technology futurist, business adviser, author, and public speaker who specializes in the areas of business strategy, global trends, and disruptive innovation. His question went a little something like this:

Imagine yourself in an oncologist's office, facing a life-altering diagnosis—cancer. You've got three choices of who, or what, will treat you.

1. A world-renowned oncologist with unmatched expertise and intuition, relying solely on their experience
2. An AI-powered physician capable of processing vast amounts of global medical data in seconds, offering unmatched precision but lacking empathy or emotional understanding
3. A skilled doctor using AI to blend human judgment with machine precision, offering personalized care while adapting to each case's nuances

Ten thousand hands raising unanimously in favor of the third option was quite a sight to see.

Each of those choices—doctor, AI, or both—reflects a different value system. And when ten thousand educators raised their hands in favor of the third option, they weren't just choosing efficiency or expertise. They were choosing empathy.

Because this isn't just a question about medicine. It's about the kind of world we're building and the kind of people we hope our students will become. Law, architecture, engineering . . . these are the careers we prepare our students to step into. And in every one of those fields, the same question lingers: When the tools get smarter, what happens to the soul of the work?

The World Economic Forum's *Future of Jobs Report* lays it out clearly: By 2030, while 92 million jobs may be displaced by automation, an estimated 170 million new ones will emerge.[17] So yes, today's kindergarteners—who likely won't retire until around the year 2090—will absolutely need to know how to collaborate with powerful AI tools we can't even imagine yet. But let's not get ahead of ourselves.

What about the roles that demand imagination? The creative paths. The human ones. The work that doesn't just solve problems but tells stories, stirs emotions, and makes meaning.

---

17 *Future of Jobs Report 2025* (World Economic Forum, 2025), https://www.weforum.org/publications/the-future-of-jobs-report-2025/.

For that, we turn to an unexpected voice from the world of storytelling itself—someone with a surprising amount of insight into the human heart in the age of AI.

Ladies and gentlemen . . . say hello to Ben Affleck.

THE CRAFTSMAN AND THE ARTIST

While medicine and education wrestle with the balance between human and machine, the world of creativity faces its own version of the same question: Can a machine ever truly understand emotion, connection, or the heart behind the work?

At CNBC's Delivering Alpha conference, Ben Affleck—yes, that Ben Affleck, of *Good Will Hunting* fame—took the stage to debut Artists Equity, a bold initiative to protect creativity and ownership in the age of AI. And while you might not think of Batman as your go-to ethics philosopher, his take was strikingly human.

Affleck isn't anti-AI. In fact, he's optimistic about its potential to make production workflows more efficient. But he draws a very clear line when it comes to art. As he puts it: "AI is a craftsman at best. . . . Craftsmen learn by imitating technique. But they're just cross-pollinating things that already exist. Nothing new is created. Craft is knowing how to work. Art is knowing when to stop. And knowing when to stop is a very difficult thing for AI to learn."[18]

That line about art is worth repeating: "Art is knowing when to stop."

How do you like *them* apples, right?

Because here's the thing: Knowing when to stop isn't just about style or structure. It's about sensing what another person might feel on the other side of the screen or the page or the classroom. It's about reading the room. Adjusting your tone. Listening for silence. Offering less when

---

[18] NBC Universal News Group, "CNBC Transcript: Ben Affleck and Gerry Cardinale Speak with CNBC's David Faber Live During the CNBC Delivering Alpha Conference Today," CNBC, November 13, 2024, https://nbcuniversalnewsgroup.com/cnbc/2024/11/13/cnbc-transcript-ben-affleck-and-gerry-cardinale-speak-with-cnbcs-david-faber-live-during-the-cnbc-delivering-alpha-conference-today/.

someone is overwhelmed. Adding more when someone feels unseen. It's about empathy.

Affleck wasn't just talking about film—he was talking about what makes us human. The best creators don't just produce; they connect. They feel their way through the work with an intuition that's built not on data but on experience, emotion, and vulnerability. That's the human edge.

As educators, our challenge mirrors this very tension. We must embrace the efficiency and possibilities of cutting-edge teaching tech without losing the heart, empathy, and creativity that define why we teach in the first place. We're not teaching to raise a generation of faceless craftsmen but to inspire the next generation of human artists. In a future where AI can bring anything we imagine to life, our classrooms must be where students learn to imagine. Because at the end of the day, people aren't moved to action when they understand; they are moved when they feel understood. And there's no better way to foster that understanding than by creating universally accessible classrooms where trust, empathy, and creativity thrive.

In our last chapter, we looked at five gamelike ways to spark creativity in any classroom. Here, let's dive into five playful strategies to bring empathy front and center in your teaching practice. These aren't just icebreakers. Each activity is a powerful tool for building trust, fostering connections, and creating a classroom culture that supports deeper, more meaningful engagement with your students, their peers, and your course content.

Whether you start the year with these activities, use them to reinvigorate a midsemester slump, or align them with a specific curricular goal, you can make every student feel seen, valued, and supported at every step of their learning journey.

These are ready to roll for any course or content area. As the old saying goes, just push play.

THROW AN UNEXPECTED CLASSROOM "SUPPLIES" PARTY

The first days of school lay the foundation for a classroom culture that lasts all year. These moments are about more than logistics; they're about creating a sense of belonging and showing students that their stories matter. And sometimes, the simplest supplies can spark the most unexpected magic. Whether it's turning a writing utensil into a yearlong badge of camaraderie or making a digital wallpaper a window into someone's world, creative uses of the everyday tools that students already bring to class can be a quirky and wildly effective way to build curiosity, collaboration, and shared respect.

There's a reason why engagement is the first pillar of UDL: Playful, intentional activities can help students connect with one another and see themselves as part of a shared journey. These activities don't require fancy resources—just a willingness to look at ordinary items in extraordinary ways.

Start the year, or any day, with Last Pen Standing, a high-energy, no-prep challenge that fosters camaraderie and accountability. Ask students to pull out the writing utensil they brought to class and give it a unique sticker. Snap a team selfie to mark the beginning of a shared journey. The challenge? See who can keep bringing the same pen or pencil to class all year long.

At random intervals throughout the days (or weeks, or months) that follow, shout "Last pen standing!" and count down from five to spark excitement and see who's still in the game. Avoid eliminating students who forgot their pen. Instead, reward points to those who remembered. It's a yearlong reminder of the power of small, consistent actions and the joy of shared memories. As a bonus, you'll be amazed at how many students start carrying an extra pen—just in case.

For a more personal twist, try Backdrop Story Swap, an activity that celebrates the stories most important to your students. Ask them to share the meaning behind their device lock screens or desktop wallpapers with a neighbor. Whether it's a picture of their pet, a favorite vacation spot, or an inspiring quote, these glimpses often spark heartfelt anecdotes and meaningful connections.

This activity can easily be adapted for schools without devices. Students can sketch a favorite memory or meaningful image to share with peers or describe the photos stored on devices kept safely in their lockers. By creating space for storytelling and listening, you foster an atmosphere of empathy and mutual respect.

Through simple activities like these, you demonstrate to students that their presence matters and their contributions shape the classroom community. Small moments like a playful challenge or a personal story lay the groundwork for a culture of curiosity, connection, and shared purpose that lasts all year long.

VIRTUAL PAINTBALL IS A GAME CHANGER

When it comes to team-based assignments, a little play can go a long way.

One of the most quoted mantras from the legendary Navy SEALs is "Slow is smooth. Smooth is fast." It's a staple of tactical maneuver manuals and training camp exercises, and it reminds us that success often begins with a clear focus on building familiarity, trust, and teamwork before jumping headlong into the fray of all kinds of unexpected challenges. And believe it or not, the US military is projected to invest over $26 billion in gamification and simulation-based training over the next three years—because playing games is a great way to get to know your team and prepare for the mission ahead.[19]

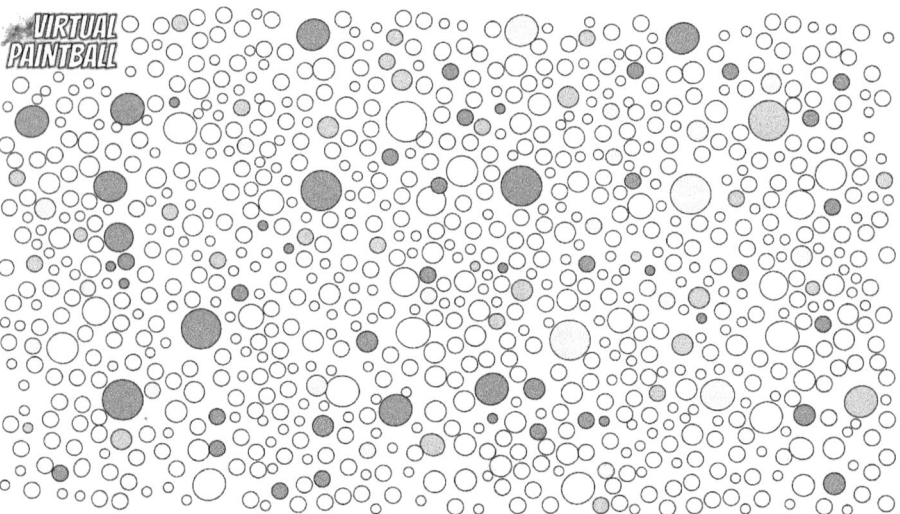

Thankfully, we don't have to spend a fortune to get our students into the teamwork game.

If you're looking to teach your students the power of working together while modeling smart, responsible, and collaborative technology use, Virtual Paintball is just what the doctor ordered! This

---

19 Alex Blair, "US Army to Spend $26bn on Gamification and Simulation Training by 2028," Army Technology, July 16, 2024, https://www.army-technology.com/news/us-army-to-spend-26bn-on-gamification-and-simulation-training-by-2028/.

fast-paced, tech-driven activity turns a simple Google Slides deck into an exciting arena for creativity, communication, and strategy.

Start by opening a blank Google Slides presentation and drawing a bunch of blank white circles across one slide as shown in the image above. Then, give the entire class shared edit access to the deck, ensuring that every student can interact with it in real time. Divide the class into color-coded teams and assign each group a unique color to represent their team.

The objective is simple: Fill in as many circles as possible with your team's color before the timer runs out (e.g., five minutes). But there's a twist. Rival teams can paint over your circles at any time, reclaiming territory for themselves! Success depends on quick thinking, constant communication, and coordinated strategies to outsmart the opposition in real time.

As the game unfolds, expect laughter, shouts of triumph, and a healthy dose of chaos as teams scramble to protect their turf while vying for new ground. The competition is fierce, but the camaraderie is even stronger.

The beauty of Virtual Paintball lies in its adaptability. Want to up the ante? Try throwing in a bunch of different shapes like triangles or stars to vary the visual challenge. Create multiple slides with different layouts and ask teams to conquer as many as possible within a set time frame. Adjust the rules to introduce new obstacles, like a total blackout variant where black-outlined circles sit on a black background. Add new goals by designating certain "power shapes" that are worth bonus points if claimed. Each variation keeps the activity fresh and engaging while challenging students to refine their strategies and collaboration skills.

After the game, bring everyone together for a reflective discussion. Ask students to share their experiences by asking questions like these:

- What strategies worked best for your team?
- How did you communicate effectively under pressure?

- Did you encounter any challenges or technical hiccups? How did you overcome them?
- How can you win without resorting to unethical tactics (like deleting entire slides)?

These reflections help students unpack the activity's lessons, reinforcing critical skills like teamwork, problem-solving, and ethical collaboration. By providing time to laugh and learn together, Virtual Paintball becomes more than a game—it's a memorable way to build trust, foster empathy, and demonstrate the power of working as a team.

GIVE STUDENTS THE CHANCE TO DO SOMETHING A-MAZE-ING TOGETHER

In today's classrooms, collaboration is more than just a buzzword—it's a vital skill for navigating the complexities of the modern world. But fostering true teamwork requires more than assigning group work; it means creating opportunities for students to step into roles, communicate effectively, and discover the unique strengths each teammate brings to the table.

One powerful way to nurture these skills is by transforming your classroom into a dynamic, team-based challenge zone. With minimal supplies—think masking tape, paper plates, or string—you can create an activity that's as engaging as it is instructive. The beauty of these challenges lies not in the materials but in the creativity and cooperation they inspire.

Picture this: Your classroom floor becomes a maze of intersecting masking tape paths. Students are divided into teams, with one blindfolded "explorer" per team tasked with navigating the maze, guided by a handful of "guides." But there's a catch—each guide can only speak a single word at a time.

The challenge begins. One guide says, "Right," another shouts, "Stop," and a third hesitates before whispering, "Forward." The explorer

takes cautious steps, trusting their teammates' fragmented directions. Laughter erupts as the explorer stumbles slightly off course, only to be steered back by the guides' carefully chosen words.

Midway through the maze, the dynamic shifts. The team realizes they need a strategy to avoid overlapping commands. The guides huddle briefly, assigning specific directional words to each member. As the explorer reaches the maze's end, cheers erupt. Together, the team reflects on what worked, what didn't, and how they adapted to the challenge.

Midgame role swaps can introduce variety, with explorers and guides switching places. Each new mission requires teams to listen, strategize, and adapt, fostering empathy and mutual respect as they navigate the maze together.

This activity isn't about the maze itself. It's about the conversations and connections it sparks. Students learn to trust one another, adapt to constraints, and communicate with clarity and purpose. The maze becomes a metaphor for life's broader challenges, emphasizing the importance of collaboration and empathy. And of course, providing time for reflection is just as important as completing the challenge. Encourage students to discuss questions like these:

- What strategies worked well for our team?
- How did we adapt to the challenges of limited communication?
- How did each teammate contribute to our success?

These discussions help students unpack their thinking routines, fostering a deeper understanding of problem-solving, decision-making, and collaboration. Articulating their experiences empowers them to apply these lessons to future challenges.

Ready to remix?

The maze can take countless forms. Use paper plates as stepping stones, challenging teams to guide their blindfolded player across the room without stepping off the stones. Or tie strings to a magic marker and have each team member hold one string, then have them collectively use their makeshift marionette to try and draw a replica of a simple image projected on the board. The possibilities are endless, each variation offering new opportunities to build teamwork and empathy.

USE (AND REUSE): A SIMPLE GRAPHIC ORGANIZER TO BUILD EMPATHY

Empathy is a cornerstone of meaningful human connection, and one of the simplest yet most impactful tools to cultivate it is the Empathy Map. This activity invites students to see the world through a different lens, whether they're analyzing a literary character, exploring the struggles of a historical figure, or stepping into the shoes of a teammate. This fosters curiosity over judgment, helping learners deepen their understanding of others' thoughts, feelings, and perspectives.

Often used in marketing and design, these maps are powerful frameworks for understanding thoughts, feelings, and motivations—but they can be transformative in the classroom. Start with a blank sheet of paper turned sideways. Draw a circle in the center (about the size of a coffee cup) and divide the page into four quadrants labeled "Seeing," "Thinking & Feeling," "Hearing," and "Saying & Doing." At the bottom, add two smaller sections: "Pain" for challenges or struggles and "Gain" for motivations or rewards.

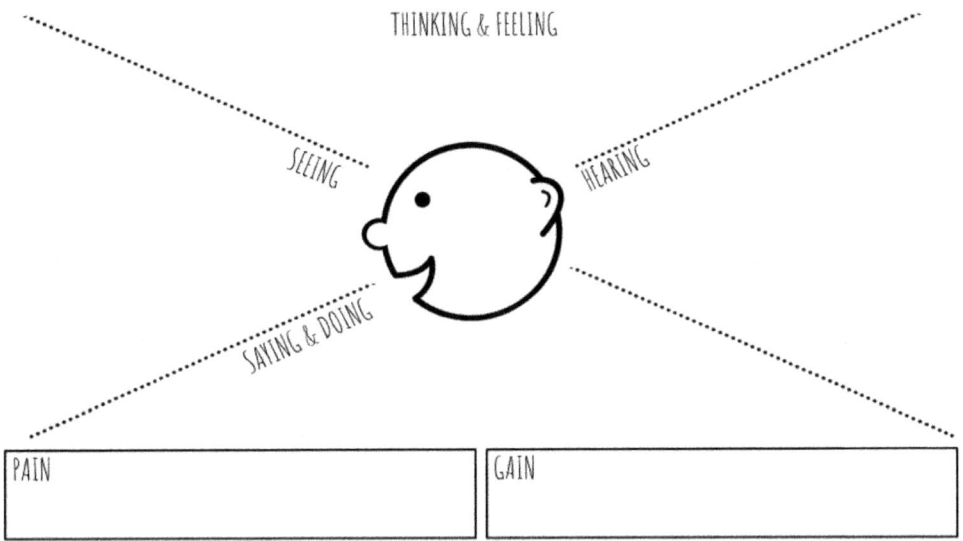

Write the name of the individual, concept, or even object you're analyzing in the center circle and start filling in bullet points for each section. With this simple setup, students can step into anyone else's shoes and gain deeper insights into their thoughts, actions, and experiences.

Empathy mapping is a natural fit for understanding a target customer, a heated political rival, or a famous character from literature—but it can also bring abstract concepts to life. Imagine these possibilities:

- What might the world look like through the eyes of a river that has witnessed the rise and fall of ancient civilizations?
- How would the square root of seven describe its place in the universe of mathematics?

By encouraging students to "become" people, places, or even inanimate objects, you unlock opportunities for humor, creativity, and connection. It's an exercise that sparks curiosity—not dismissive judgment—and helps students view the world from perspectives they may never have considered.

Once students get the feel for the activity, the Empathy Map activity can also serve as a lead-in to class-wide dialogues or Socratic seminars. Students can step deeper into their roles as historical figures, literary characters, or abstract concepts and participate in discussions while staying in character. This approach not only deepens their understanding of diverse viewpoints but also makes these discussions more engaging and less confrontational, even when tackling challenging topics.

This activity teaches critical skills like perspective-taking, self-awareness, and collaboration. It provides a structured yet safe framework for exploring diverse viewpoints, sparking insights and creativity that enrich every student's learning experience. Whether used to dive deeper into course content or as a springboard for meaningful class discussions, the Empathy Map builds a foundation of understanding that transcends the classroom.

THEMED WORK MAKES THE TEAM WORK

Theming isn't just about making activities more fun; it's a powerful way to foster teamwork, communication, and problem-solving in the classroom. By wrapping challenges in engaging, high-stakes scenarios, you help students step into imaginative roles, tackle unique problems, and experience the thrill of working together under pressure. One standout example of this is a themed simulation we like to call Pipeline Panic, where your students are thrust into a critical mission to save the day.

Here's the skinny.

Disaster has struck. A devastating oil spill (a.k.a. about a dozen ping-pong balls, each marked with a simple X) is threatening the safety of marine life in a nearby bay. Your class has been recruited as an elite team of rescue engineers tasked with building an emergency pipeline to divert the oil and deliver clean water to save the ecosystem. Supplies are scarce, the clock is ticking, and failure is not an option. Armed with limited resources—cardboard tubes, duct tape, scissors, and a handful of other materials—teams must construct a pipeline strong enough to carry clean water (represented by ping-pong balls without any "X" markings on them) from the starting point to the endpoint without spilling or breaking along the way.

On your marks. Get set. Go!

The room becomes a hive of activity as students brainstorm, test, and adapt their designs in real time.

To succeed, teams need to communicate effectively, assign roles, and solve problems collaboratively under pressure. The pipeline must meet specific design criteria: It must be structurally sound and able to transport the appropriately marked ping-pong balls across a designated distance; each section of the pipeline must connect seamlessly, requiring careful planning and precision; and the entire build must be completed in a fixed amount of time—perhaps twenty minutes—adding a layer of urgency to the challenge. Along the way, unexpected obstacles may arise at your discretion. Perhaps a critical junction springs a leak, the classroom lights go out and students must work in total darkness, or a sudden "storm" introduced by the teacher forces teams to rework a section of their pipeline as additional obstacles (like a few more ping-pong balls marked with the dreaded X) are added into the simulation. These silly twists heighten the stakes, encouraging students to stay flexible and think on their feet.

Once the challenge is complete, teams gather to test their pipelines and see if their designs hold up. Success is celebrated, but even failures become invaluable learning experiences. A debriefing session follows, with students reflecting on their performance. What strategies worked best for their team? How did they overcome setbacks or disagreements? What would they do differently next time? These discussions allow students to unpack their thinking, recognize the value of teamwork, and identify areas for improvement.

This activity can also serve as a springboard for creativity. Once students have experienced Pipeline Panic, invite them to design their own themed challenges. Could they create a mission to build a bridge strong enough to carry precious cargo across a perilous canyon? Or devise a system to rescue endangered animals trapped in a forest fire? Let their imaginations run wild, using ordinary materials to craft extraordinary scenarios where teamwork and problem-solving take center stage.

Themed activities aren't just a simple diversion—they're immersive, unforgettable experiences that elevate a simple engineering challenge into a memorable lesson in collaboration, empathy, and critical thinking. By framing the activity as a daring team-based rescue mission, you make the stakes feel tangible. This type of challenge shows how ordinary materials and creative storytelling can turn the classroom into an environment where collaboration thrives and challenges feel exciting and meaningful. While the stakes may be fictional, the skills students develop—clear communication, role delegation, and resilience under pressure—are very real.

CHEATER, CHEATER, PUMPKIN EATER

Since we've devoted so much time in this chapter to reaffirming our humanity and building trust in our classrooms, now feels like as good a time as any to ask something difficult: What happens when that trust is called into question? And what happens when we let machines, rather than people, be the ones to judge student efforts?

For busy teachers already teetering on the brink of burnout, automated scoring tools have long been a lifesaver. Trusty Scantron machines and plagiarism checkers like Turnitin.com lighten the load, making it possible to grade massive stacks of assignments with relative ease. And in the era of AI? It's easier than ever to streamline the grading process. Edtech tools can analyze student work in seconds, offering breakdowns of strengths, weaknesses, and even ready-to-enter scores. There's also been a boom in AI detection software, promising to catch any traces of machine-assisted writing at the push of a button.

Pretty cool, right?

But here's the thing: Efficiency isn't always foolproof. What happens when one of these tools gets it wrong? And what happens when a student who poured their heart into an assignment is accused of letting a bot do the heavy lifting? These questions force us to think carefully about how we balance trust, efficiency, and fairness in the AI era.

Teaching is, at its core, a profoundly human endeavor. And we need to tread carefully when we embrace AI tools for our own benefit only to turn around and tell students they can't do the same.

If Ben Affleck was right, at its best, AI can function like a craftsperson. It can analyze patterns, detect statistical anomalies, and follow programmed rules. But it will never be an artist. It will never understand the fear, pressure, or quiet victories behind each student's work.

In fact, new research by the Center for Democracy and Technology reveals just how deeply AI has woven itself into students' academic lives. During the 2023 to 2024 school year, upward of 70 percent of high school students admitted to using AI in their studies (let's note that the key word here is *admit*). This was up from 58 percent the previous year. Yet 1 in 5 students said they or someone they know was accused of relying on AI to cheat on an assignment without proof or when it was later concluded that no inappropriate use of AI had occurred. At the same time, 39 percent of teachers reported regularly using AI content detection software to manage students' AI use, despite many lacking clear guidance on handling suspected plagiarism. This dynamic highlights a troubling hypocrisy: While educators rely on AI to lighten their workload, students often face suspicion—or outright accusations—for doing the exact same thing.[20]

So, good for the goose but not for the gander?

All of this plays out against the backdrop of what feels like a technological tango—a never-ending game of cat and mouse click with students using AI tools to create and teachers deploying AI tools to detect. The rapid evolution of AI tech means that students now even have access to tools designed to help them cover their tracks, adding yet another layer of absurdity to the cycle.

---

20 Anna Merod, "Student, Teacher AI Use Continued to Climb in 2023–24 School Year," K–12 Dive, January 15, 2025, https://www.k12dive.com/news/student-teacher-ai-use-schools-cdt/737335/.

This gap presents both a challenge and an opportunity for educators. If AI is already shaping the way students learn, how can we reimagine our classrooms to meet them where they are? What if instead of using AI to police dishonesty, we used it to foster collaboration, build trust, and design assessments that showcase students' humanity?

Machines can process data, but they can't replace the ghost in the machine—the trust, empathy, and human connection that make teaching truly meaningful. Because when we start outsourcing judgment to algorithms, when we let AI dictate who we trust and who we don't . . .

That's when the machine stops serving our students and starts ghosting us all.

Teachers using AI to catch students suspected of using AI feels dystopian—almost absurd. And each time we call a student into our room to say, "I think you cheated on this assignment," aren't we also saying, "I think you're the type of person who would cheat"?

For a student, being accused of cheating isn't just a question of academic integrity. It's a question of character. Hearing that accusation from a trusted teacher can be devastating. It's a sad reality that plays out too often in classrooms around the world, eroding the bonds of trust that are essential to the teacher-student relationship.

So what if instead of replacing trust with surveillance, we reimagined our assessments altogether? What if we designed learning experiences so engaging, immersive, and distinctly human that AI-generated work simply couldn't compete?

And with a one-two punch of UDL and playful pedagogy, imagine creating assignments so engaging and immersive that students wouldn't even consider cheating. These challenges would demand not just content knowledge but the unique spark of their own ideas.

Now let's turn all this theory into practice.

A PLAYBOOK FOR EMPATHY

At the heart of every strategy in this chapter is a simple, profound message to our students: You matter. Today is fundamentally different because you showed up. I'm really glad you're here today, and I can't wait to see you again tomorrow.

When we communicate this sentiment, we create classrooms where empathy, creativity, and trust can thrive.

In the previous chapter, we explored how a touch of creativity and gamelike elements can transform our classrooms into hubs of engagement and joy. Now, we're taking that same spirit of innovation and applying it to assessments, reimagining them as opportunities to deepen connections between students, their peers, and the material they're learning.

Let's take a look!

GET TO KNOW ME EMPATHY MAPS

Game On

Transform one-on-one meetings into meaningful and imaginative experiences with Get to Know Me Empathy Maps! This dynamic graphic organizer helps teachers uncover each student's unique interests, strengths, and needs across academic, social-emotional, and career domains. Whether used as a conversation starter during goal setting or reimagined digitally, this activity helps build trust, empathy, and actionable goals. Want to take it a step further? Use AI tools to generate personalized visuals of these students stepping into their dream roles. You're giving them the chance to literally see themselves as an astronaut, an archaeologist, or anything they can imagine!

An Empathetic Upgrade

With traditional student surveys or goal-setting templates, conversations sometimes feel generic or one-sided. This activity greatly improves the student experience.

Quick-Start Guide

1. **Prepare blank empathy maps:** Include sections for interests and goals, areas of strength, academic needs, SEL needs, and career needs as shown in the image below.
2. **Meet with students:** This can be done individually or in small groups. Encourage them to share what excites them, challenges them, and inspires their dreams as they fill out their maps.
3. **Use AI:** If a student dreams of becoming a globe-trotting archaeologist, use AI to create a fun, fictionalized version of that journey. Remember that privacy is paramount, and it doesn't need to be them—just someone like them, living out that dream. These kinds of visuals can spark motivation and keep future goals top of mind.

Pedagogy Power-Up

Hang on to these completed empathy maps and refer to them often to help inform future lessons where you can better account for differentiated instruction, build stronger student-teacher connections, and design even more personalized learning pathways. For a classroom twist, have peers exchange maps to discuss common interests or collaboratively brainstorm ways to support each other's goals.

House Rules

AI isn't just for generating visuals—it can even assist in refining goals or identifying pathways to success. Consider dedicating a full student-teacher conference to a one-on-one (plus one!) meeting where an AI tool joins you and your student at the table as a virtual sounding board. As you and your student get comfortable sharing this information with the bot, give them the opportunity to see how AI can help them brainstorm steps to achieve their dreams, providing practical advice or even creating short scripts for future career scenarios.

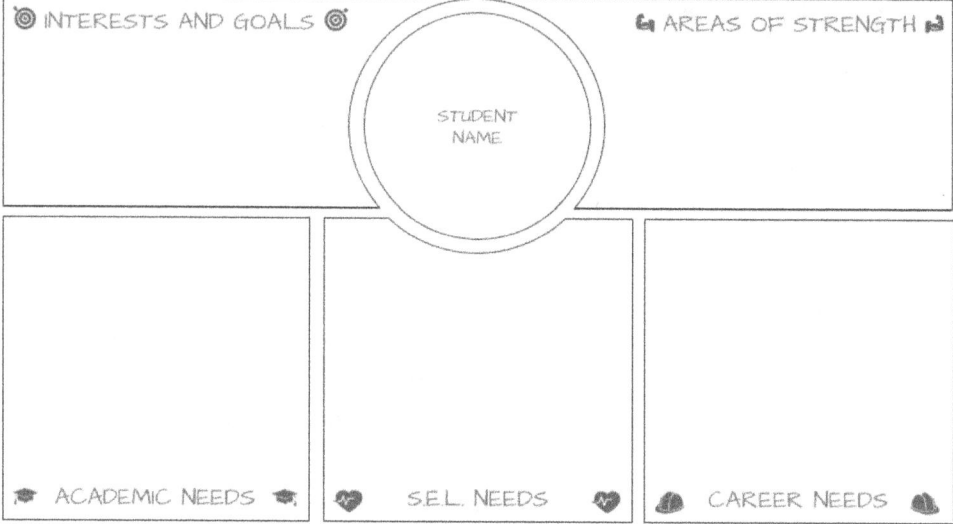

UDL for the Win

This activity aligns beautifully with all three UDL principles, offering students meaningful ways to connect with their learning and each other.

- **Engagement** (the *why* of learning): This activity creates a safe space for students to reflect on what excites them and what challenges they face, fostering curiosity and connection. Revisiting the maps throughout the year builds trust and ensures students feel seen, valued, and motivated.
- **Representation** (the *what* of learning): The clear structure of the map—divided into interests, strengths, and needs—makes it accessible for all learners. Visual prompts and options for verbal or written participation allow students to engage in ways that work best for them.

- **Action and expression** (the *how* of learning): Students can complete the maps individually or collaborate with peers to share insights. Periodic updates to the maps encourage reflection on growth, helping students track their evolving interests and goals.

STORYTELLING WITH SCRABBLE

Game On

Transform the classic game of Scrabble into a powerful tool for self-expression! Students use all one hundred tiles—or as many as they can—to fill the board with words that tell their unique story. And since we're making up new rules for a more inclusive way to play, they are free to spell words in any direction, even upside down or backward, as long as every word connects to something meaningful about them. Whether they're sharing hobbies, dreams, favorite memories, or quirks, students will surprise you with how much they reveal when serious work feels like anything but.

Want to go beyond the personal? Revisit this activity later in the year to introduce and review curricular topics or reflect on unit themes.

An Empathetic Upgrade

This is way better than generic icebreakers or "tell me about yourself" worksheets that lack creative flair.

Quick-Start Guide

1. **Set up the board:** Provide students with a Scrabble game board (physical or virtual at PlayScrabble.com). Explain that they can use as many tiles as possible to create a word-based mosaic that describes who they are, what they value, or what excites them.
2. **Build connections:** Encourage students to weave their words together, just like in traditional Scrabble, but with no rigid

scoring rules. Focus on creativity, not competition. Give students the freedom to form words upside down and backward if they'd like, but make it known that every word must reflect something personal, like hobbies (LACROSSE), emotions (JOY), or aspirations (ROADTRIP).

3. **Score (optional):** If you'd like, score the board as usual. However, the main goal is self-expression, not a high score (though many students love competing against themselves to see if they can lock in maximum points).

4. **Reflect and share:** Once finished, students can present their boards to small groups or the class, explaining why certain words matter to them. Take photos of these completed projects and save them in a shared file, or give your students the opportunity to share their stories in private, one-on-one conversations with you as you see fit.

Pedagogy Power-Up

Storytelling with Scrabble creates a safe and playful space for students to express themselves. It builds empathy and helps teachers discover common threads across the class. For a more meaningful connection, revisit these boards at key milestones (e.g., before parent-teacher conferences or end-of-year reflections) to track personal growth.

House Rules

Save time and reduce setup effort by directing students to PlayScrabble.com for an instant digital board. Pair this activity with AI tools to enrich discussions. Use ChatGPT to generate prompts for students who may need inspiration or to craft narratives based on the words they've chosen.

> **Pro tip:** AI tools can even help translate student boards into poetry or short creative essays, bringing their words to life in new formats.

UDL for the Win

Storytelling with Scrabble engages students by turning self-expression into a game. It supports representation through diverse options for creating word mosaics and enables action and expression with flexible presentation formats.

- **Engagement** (the *why* of learning): The playful, low-pressure format encourages creativity and curiosity, making self-expression feel fun and meaningful. Revisiting the activity throughout the year helps reinforce its relevance and keeps students motivated.
- **Representation** (the *what* of learning): The game's mechanics are intuitive and adaptable, offering multiple entry points for learners to craft sentences or design visual boards. Scaffolding options, like prompts or sample boards, ensure accessibility for all.
- **Action and expression** (the *how* of learning): Students can share their word mosaics through presentations, gallery walks, or peer discussions. The reflective element invites them to articulate their stories and connect with others meaningfully.

STICKER SWAG SOIREE

Game On
Let your students' personalities shine with a Sticker Swag Soiree! Your students may have laptops covered in stickers already, or perhaps your school requires devices to stay clean. Either way, this activity is adaptable and bursting with creative potential. Students with decorated laptops can share the stories behind their stickers, while those with blank devices (or loaners) can design the laptop cover of their dreams using a blank slideshow.

An Empathetic Upgrade
This replaces boring back-to-school conversations that don't spark creativity or connection.

Quick-Start Guide

1. **Tell the story:** Students with laptop stickers can showcase their swag, sharing the personal stories or meaning behind each design. Encourage them to explain how their stickers reflect their passions, hobbies, or quirks.
2. **Dream up laptop designs:** If students don't already have decorated laptops, no worries! Provide them with a blank digital slide (PowerPoint or Google Slides work perfectly) or an old-school printed outline of a laptop case (a.k.a. a blank sheet of paper). Invite them to use this blank canvas as the backdrop for all kinds of "stickers" that showcase their personality, interests, and values.
3. **Go no tech or high-tech:** Bust out the magic markers and colored pencils to give students the chance to explore themes, symbols, or images that resonate with who they are, or use free AI-powered tools to help them turn ordinary online photos into sleek virtual stickers.

4. **Share the swag:** Once the stickers are created or showcased, students can present their designs in small groups or as part of a classroom gallery walk. Encourage them to talk about why certain stickers represent who they are and what matters to them.

Pedagogy Power-Up

This activity provides a low-pressure, high-creativity way for students to share their stories and build classroom connections. It's also a great exercise in storytelling and visual expression.

Pro tip: Once your learners have gotten the hang of this activity, feel free to revisit your Sticker Swag Soiree throughout the year by incorporating content themes related to your latest unit of study. What might Marie Curie's laptop have looked like? Or Martin Luther King Jr.'s? Use this activity as an ongoing creative outlet, giving your students a familiar space where they can reflect on curriculum topics.

House Rules

Make the design process easier and more engaging with AI tools that don't require registration. Teach students how to use free online AI tools like Remove.bg or graphic design suites like Canva and Photoshop Express. These have the power to turn any online image into a clean, background-free .png file, perfect for creating virtual stickers of their designs.

UDL for the Win

Sticker Swag Soiree engages students with a creative outlet for personal expression. It supports representation through multimodal design options and enables action and expression by letting students share their stories in diverse ways.

- **Engagement** (the *why* of learning): This activity encourages students to reflect on their identity and passions, sparking joy and curiosity. Revisiting the activity with curriculum themes builds relevance and keeps engagement high.
- **Representation** (the *what* of learning): Students can express themselves with stickers, drawings, or digital tools, providing multiple pathways for creativity. Prompts like "What image represents your favorite memory?" ensure participation for all.
- **Action and expression** (the *how* of learning): Students can showcase their designs in small groups, gallery walks, or digital presentations. The iterative process of creating and reflecting deepens understanding and builds connections with peers.

QUESTIONS FOR DISCUSSION

1. Daniel Burrus's thought experiment highlights the importance of blending human intuition with technological precision. Reflecting on your own teaching practice, where do you see opportunities to integrate technology without losing the human element? What steps can you take to ensure that empathy and connection remain at the heart of your instruction?
2. Ben Affleck's assertion that "art is knowing when to stop" underscores the limits of AI in replacing true human creativity. How can you design classroom experiences that encourage students to develop their unique voices and creativity, even as they engage with AI tools? Where might you find a balance between efficiency and fostering authentic expression?
3. This chapter challenges us to rethink traditional assessments, moving away from tools that police dishonesty and toward tasks that inspire curiosity and creativity. How might you redesign one of your current assessments to better celebrate student ideas, foster trust, and make cheating an irrelevant option?

*ALMOST ALL CREATIVITY
INVOLVES PURPOSEFUL PLAY.*

ABRAHAM MASLOW

CHAPTER 4

PLAY WITH PURPOSE

GAMIFICATION AS A LEARNING FLYWHEEL

Ciao, everyone! Michael here. And I love games.

There's just something extraordinary about a great game. The best ones suck us in, ignite our curiosity, and challenge us to think and adapt. They create worlds that captivate us, moments that matter, and experiences that stick with us long after the game ends. But what exactly makes a game amazing? And why did I want to bring that excitement into the classroom?

I've always been fascinated by the way games create unrivaled engagement. When I was a kid, my favorite night of the year was Christmas Eve. This wasn't about what the morning would bring; it was about what our family friends Carrie and Len Touney, along with their three kids, would bring that night.

Our families were inseparable, and every year, we packed into one house like a big blended family. Carrie loved games, and she loved me; she was like my second mother. Each Christmas Eve, she would arrive with a brand-new game—usually a party game, something none of us had played before. We'd crack it open that night and dive in together. The room would fill with laughter, friendly chaos, and the kind of joy that only comes from being completely present in the moment.

A few years ago, Carrie passed away, but I will never forget those nights or her love of games. Every time I pull up a chair, pick up a piece, and play, I think of her.

In high school, I'd get lost for hours in epic global battles of Axis & Allies and Diplomacy with friends. Whether I was rolling dice, solving puzzles, or plotting the perfect move, games weren't just entertainment—they challenged me to think in new ways and push beyond what I thought I could do. And as I grew older, I realized something profound: Games aren't just fun. They are powerful.

The best games do something exceptional—they make us care. They tap into what it means to be human through curiosity, competition, and creativity. They create a situation where failure isn't a stop sign but a stepping stone, where every challenge is an opportunity, and where players are driven to keep trying and improving. The best games transform us from passive participants into active, invested players.

When I became a teacher, I quickly realized that the traditional classroom wasn't always built with this same spirit in mind. Too often, learning felt like something students had to endure rather than something they got to experience. Worksheets replaced wonder. Textbooks took the place of trials. And worst of all, failure felt like a final judgment instead of a natural and essential part of growth.

That's when it clicked. What if we could take the power of games—the engagement, the excitement, the drive—and bring that into learning?

Not all games are created equal, and that's an important truth to remember. Just because something has points or a leaderboard doesn't automatically make it a great game. A well-designed game isn't just about mechanics; it's about meaning. The best games create a sense of purpose, connection, and mastery. They are about more than winning. They're about growth, discovery, and storytelling.

Gamification, when done right, doesn't just make learning more fun; it makes it more meaningful. It's like a flywheel: Once you get the thing turning, each small win adds momentum. Before long, you've got a classroom running on curiosity, challenge, and connection, with students pushing themselves to keep the wheel spinning.

This is why I gamify. Not because I want students to be entertained but because I want them to be engaged. I want them to feel the rush of solving a tough problem, the camaraderie of working together, and the thrill of taking on a challenge and coming out stronger. I want to

transform the classroom into a space where learning feels like an epic quest, where every student is a hero, every challenge is an opportunity, and every failure is just another step on the path to mastery.

The best games don't just change the way we play. They change the way we think, learn, and ultimately see the world. And if we can harness even a fraction of that power in our classrooms, we can transform education into something truly unforgettable.

DO NOT PASS GO

In chapter 1, we took aim at the brightly colored button-mashing giants of gamified edtech, such as Kahoot! But when it comes to bad game role models, they're far from the only culprits.

Take Monopoly, for example. The best-selling board game in the world has likely found its way onto your table at least once. As a shared cultural touchstone, that's not necessarily a bad thing. But Monopoly is riddled with serious design flaws, and for many, it's the quintessential example of everything wrong with gaming. Moreover, this famous but flawed board game may even discourage educators from exploring the universally engaging potential of playful pedagogy in their classrooms, casting games as shallow, frustrating, or ineffective tools for learning.

But here's the thing: Gamification isn't about reducing rigor. It's about amplifying it. Done right, games can be transformative, turning learning into an active, engaging, and meaningful experience. The key is knowing what not to emulate—and Monopoly is a perfect place to start.

Here are five big lessons that teachers can learn from Monopoly's missteps.

1. **Don't spend more time waiting than playing.** Monopoly's pacing issues are a perfect storm of disengagement. Players spend more time waiting than participating, and as turns drag on, early excitement fizzles into boredom. In UDL terms, this

is a red flag for engagement, which thrives on active involvement and novelty. Great classroom games eliminate downtime by keeping all students engaged in meaningful tasks, balancing moments of intensity with opportunities to reflect or strategize. Momentum is the cornerstone of any engaging activity. Without it, the entire structure collapses.

2. **When luck overpowers strategy, learning stalls.** In Monopoly, a roll of the dice often determines success, leaving players powerless to shape their outcomes. This reliance on luck robs players of meaningful decisions and stifles their ability to think critically. In UDL terms, it undermines the action and expression principle, which emphasizes giving students multiple ways to demonstrate their understanding and creativity. Classroom games should empower learners to make strategic choices, experiment with ideas, and take risks. By shifting the focus to thoughtful decision-making, we help students build the scaffolding for deeper learning.

3. **Games should be fair and inclusive.** Monopoly's elimination mechanics and bad rolls exclude players and create unnecessary barriers to participation. And when you try to add house rules (like scoring a windfall of cash for landing on Free Parking), you actually end up making the game even worse! This design flaw highlights another critical UDL principle: equity. Barriers exist in systems, not in students. Classroom games must remove these obstacles by ensuring all learners have access to meaningful roles and pathways to success. Inclusive design ensures every student can contribute, fostering a sense of belonging and strengthening the collaborative foundation of the learning experience.

4. **Soft skills are the mortar of strong learning.** Fancy vocab words and the usual array of facts and figures might be the bricks of every curriculum, but without collaboration—the mortar—your structure is destined to crumble. Monopoly's

zero-sum approach to competition pits players against each other and discourages teamwork, reinforcing a mindset of isolation. In contrast, UDL emphasizes collaboration and representation, encouraging students to work together, communicate, and build on each other's strengths. By layering soft skills like teamwork and communication into classroom games, we ensure the learning foundation is sturdy and ready to weather any storm.

5. **Complexity doesn't equal depth.** Monopoly's convoluted rules (auctions, mortgages, and themed variations) add layers of confusion without delivering deeper engagement. Trying to explain all these mechanics to a new player often feels like asking them to drink from a firehose. This complexity doesn't lead to depth or mastery but to frustration and disengagement. In UDL terms, it's a missed opportunity for representation, which calls for clear, accessible tasks that allow students to focus on exploration and creativity rather than mechanics. Classroom games don't need to be overly complicated to be effective. The best designs are simple yet rich with opportunities for curiosity, problem-solving, and mastery. By keeping mechanics intuitive, we help students invest more energy into learning and less into deciphering the game itself.

In Monopoly, we see a perfect storm of design flaws that make games frustrating, disengaging, and ultimately ineffective for learning. Facing the thought of excessive downtime, luck-based mechanics, and a lack of creativity and collaboration, it's easy to understand why so many educators hesitate to bring games into their classrooms. If this is what games are, they seem at odds with deep learning and meaningful engagement.

But they don't have to be.

So let's take a closer look at what really goes into great game design. Then we'll use what we've learned to help our schools build a better mousetrap. Er . . . horse, that is.

CRAFTING A PLAYFUL CLASSROOM BRICK BY BRICK

Wanna know a secret?

Gamification isn't trickery—but like a Trojan horse, it can disarm resistance and invite students to engage more deeply than they might initially realize. When it's done right, gamification is a powerful design tool that turns passive students into active learners.

At first glance, it all looks like fun and games—an engaging diversion from the so-called serious work of education. But that's the secret: Purposeful play and gamification are anything but fluff. When intentionally designed, they unleash a transformative power, igniting curiosity, fostering collaboration, and making even the most complex subjects feel accessible and exciting.

And we're not the only ones who think so.

Just look at LEGO, the playful juggernaut that has been shaping minds and imaginations for over seventy years. With a staggering $13 billion valuation (yes, with a *b*!), the company has invested heavily in researching what truly works in learning environments. While most teachers don't have access to a LEGO-sized R&D budget, we can tap into what the company's findings reveal about crafting more engaging, impactful classroom experiences.

LEGO's "State of Classroom Engagement Report," based on insights from over six thousand educators, parents, and students, reveals a simple but powerful truth: Play creates classrooms where learning feels so intuitive, joyful, and irresistible that students can't wait to share what they've discovered.[21] Imagine a world where "How was school today?" consistently sparks animated, enthusiastic responses. According to LEGO's research, this isn't just a pipe dream—it's very much within reach.

Unfortunately, only about one-third of educators, parents, and administrators describe students as "genuinely engaged" in learning. This lack of engagement doesn't just affect academic performance;

---

21 LEGO, "State of Classroom Engagement Report," September 4, 2024, https://education.lego.com/en-us/classroom-engagement-report/.

it's tied to absenteeism, behavioral issues, and low confidence. These challenges ripple through classrooms and communities, but LEGO's research highlights bold solutions that can reverse these trends and reenergize learning environments.

Play, as LEGO points out, is one of those solutions. Hands-on, collaborative activities allow students to connect socially while deepening their understanding of the material. When kids work together to solve problems or build something tangible, they don't just learn—they engage. They experience the thrill of creativity and the satisfaction of mastering challenges.

And it's not just about test scores (although it helps there too). LEGO's report shows that engaged students are four times as likely to be happy and five times as likely to feel confident versus their disengaged peers. That means less cheating. Lower absentee rates. Higher test scores. And more time spent directly on whatever task happens to be assigned. Teachers benefit, too, reporting higher job satisfaction when their students thrive.

When learning feels like play, everyone wins.

Playful learning isn't limited to kindergartners stacking colorful blocks. Older students crave hands-on, interactive experiences that connect abstract concepts to real-world scenarios. Yet opportunities for play often dwindle as students age, crowded out by rigid curricula and standardized testing. LEGO emphasizes that play doesn't have to mean chaos. Structured exploration and purposeful collaboration create a kind of joyful messiness—what the celebrated psychologist Mihaly Csikszentmihalyi famously identified as the elusive state of *flow*, where students lose themselves in challenges that perfectly match their skills.

And yes, LEGO might be in the business of selling us sets of plastic building blocks. But play isn't a toy set—it's a *mindset*. It tricks us (and our students) into working harder, thinking deeper, and sticking with challenges longer than we otherwise might. It sneaks into the classroom under the guise of fun and unleashes something far greater. As LEGO so aptly puts it, "The path to increased engagement is paved in purposeful play."[22] By embracing play, we can create classrooms where students and teachers rediscover the joy of learning—and leave every day feeling like they've built something amazing.

So let's pick up the pieces—or whatever tools we can imagine—and start building classrooms full of energy, curiosity, and meaningful play. Because believe it or not, creating that kind of engagement really is as easy as one, two, three . . .

Step 1: Put an End to Button Mashing

Here's how you build a bad classroom game: The teacher divides students into competing teams. Each team appoints a single player to represent them. The teacher asks a review question to both groups. The first student to buzz in with the correct answer wins a point for their team, and their opponent is left feeling absolutely worthless. The student goes back to their group and tries to avoid the awkward stares of their teammates or the haunting chorus of their inner monologue, echoing with some serious negative self-talk.

Here's how you build a better classroom game: Theme. Teams. Tasks.

- **Select a theme**: No need to reinvent the wheel! Simply select a theme that's inspired by your current unit of study. Perhaps your students are racing to find a cure for a newly discovered disease. Or they're sent back deep into the pages of history to uncover the dark secrets of a shadowy usurper's kingdom. Teaching a more abstract concept and stuck for a theme? AI tools like ChatGPT are your friend.
- **Divide into teams:** Amplify the immersion by selecting (or having students select) names inspired by the world in which you set your game. If you're racing to find a cure, then each student group is a globe-trotting scientist. If you're trekking through history, perhaps they're time-traveling archaeologists.

---
22 Ibid.

- **Assign tasks:** This is every teacher's bread and butter. Design meaningful tasks that help students show what they know. The catch here is simply to select tasks that are *variable* in nature and *infinite* in the number of correct answers. Let's see what we mean in step 2.

Step 2: Embrace the Open-Ended Power of UDL

The teacher divides students into competing teams and assigns each of them the exact same task. "Working with your teammates, you'll have the chance to draw a giant picture that incorporates as many details from the textbook as you can find. Be creative and talk it out as you go! This might not be an art class, but feel free to use as much color and detail as you can. Dig through your textbooks and find as many examples of [topic] to include in your picture as you can. You have ten minutes. Be prepared to explain your decisions, and make sure to include page numbers!"

Perhaps this is an elementary school science class, with competing teams sketching photos of a unit on undersea life. Maybe it's a middle school social studies class making multiple copies of an action-packed timeline of their favorite battle in the American Revolution. Or how about an AP English classroom with rival squads pulling in all sorts of text evidence to illustrate the differences between life in the big city and life on the raft in Mark Twain's *Adventures of Huckleberry Finn*.

The fundamental gameplay is the same regardless of who is playing. And note how we don't challenge students to be the first team to come up with five examples. Instead, we ask them to take ten minutes and find as many examples as they can. When time runs out? Ask students to review their lists, working together with their teammates to select what they believe to be the three very best submissions to share with their classmates.

Metacognition for the win.

Step 3: Build an Army of Activities Your Students Will Love

Suddenly, everybody on each team has an equal chance to contribute at the same time. You've got a perpetual motion machine of artists, researchers, readers, decision-makers, and student presenters working together for the duration of the game. Teams are a flurry of activity throughout the competition, and you have the chance to float between groups offering positive feedback on the spot—giving every student the chance to take pride in the work that they are doing.

No more one-sided runaways. No more dead time waiting for other teams to take their turn. Excitement right down to the wire. Rapt attention as team after team turns their eyes away from their own creations to soak in the greatest hits of what their classmates have made. That epic finale moment when it all comes down to one tiny detail and you (the judge) get to make the call. Or better yet, this is a chance for all students to vote on which team they think deserves the win. Have them explain why! There's a very real chance any and every player can walk away from the game feeling like they were the MVP.

Want to play again? Heck yes! "All right, gang—we'll do this again tomorrow. Make sure to read chapter 2 for homework!"

And just like that, the energy is through the roof. Everyone walks away feeling seen, heard, valued, and validated. And once students know that their efforts will be on display for their peers, the quality of their work inevitably climbs higher with each passing day.

The rising tide lifts all ships.

ENGAGEMENT ENGINEERS IN ACTION

When you know where to look, gamification is everywhere. It's on Starbucks apps, nudging us to collect stars for a free cup of coffee. It's in fitness watches, encouraging us to meet our daily goals. It powers frequent-flier promotions and online shopping carts, enticing us to make just one more purchase. Even our streaming platforms use gamification, analyzing our viewing habits to keep us hooked for "just one more episode" of the latest binge-worthy series. Whether it's driving customer loyalty or boosting engagement, gamification has become a cornerstone of industries worldwide. In fact, nearly three-quarters of the world's largest companies use its principles to attract customers, increase profits, and influence behavior.[23]

See, gamification doesn't mean playing full-fledged games. Instead, it's about adapting the elements that make our favorite games so addictive and applying those same principles to the world outside of gaming.

Gamified systems captivate us because they blend choice with challenge, balance feedback with failure, and reward evolving strategies and skills. They keep us coming back, smarter and more determined after every win (or loss). Whether we're scoring virtual high fives on a Peloton ride or joining a charity campaign to unlock a matching gift, gamification celebrates our successes and invites others to play along. It challenges us to take risks, try new approaches, and find joy in the process—all while making us feel like part of something bigger than ourselves.

When paired with thoughtful design principles like UDL, gamification celebrates strategic play while creating universal appeal. It isn't frivolous; it's a design strategy for serious learning.

James Paul Gee, a leading researcher at the intersection of play and literacy, shows how video games offer a blueprint for how humans learn best—through active, meaningful experiences. In *Portal*, for example, players explore physics not by memorizing formulas but by experimenting with gravity and velocity in a virtual world. This messy, trial-and-error approach to learning gives rise to what Gee calls affinity spaces, where players collaborate in massive online communities, using vast tomes of specialist vocabulary directly inspired by their shared experiences. Concepts that might have seemed overwhelmingly complex in a textbook can feel downright intuitive when learned in the immersive context of the game world.

---

23 "Exploring the Widespread Use of Gamification Across Various Industries," Spinify, accessed September 25, 2025," https://spinify.com/blog/world-renowned-companies-using-gamification-successfully/.

Gee humorously recounts his first attempt at video games as an overwhelmed boomer who tried to master them by reading the manual. Predictably, it didn't work. But after hours of trial and error, the once-impenetrable language of the manual became crystal clear. His takeaway? Schools often give students "the manuals without the games"—abstract concepts without real-world connections.[24] Expecting students to master math or science without engaging with its practical applications is like handing gamers a rule book and expecting them to win. Instead, educators should let students "play" first—tinker, explore, and experiment—so the "manuals" can intuitively make a lot more sense.

That's the beauty of gamification. It turns passive learning into a flywheel of purposeful play—one that spins faster and stronger with every challenge, every collaboration, and every win.

What follows are a few examples of how playful design and thoughtful gamification can ignite curiosity, foster collaboration, and inspire creativity for learners of all ages. These stories highlight the innovative ways educators are integrating these principles into their classrooms, creating learning experiences that are intuitive, purposeful, and immersive. Let's explore how a few dedicated teachers are leveraging resources we've made available to the EMC² Learning community to transform their classrooms into vibrant spaces of engagement and discovery.

E KOMO MAI TO A HIGH SCHOOLER'S PEER REVIEW PARADISE

In Kathleen Mathis's high school English classroom in Annandale, Virginia, peer review is more than an academic exercise—it's an adventure. Inspired by the spirit of collaboration and playful engagement, she transformed her classroom into Peer Review Paradise, a vibrant island-hopping activity that paid tribute to her Polynesian heritage while inviting students to explore their peers' writing in a whole new way.

---

[24] "James Paul Gee on Learning with Video Games," Edutopia, posted March 21, 2012, YouTube, https://www.youtube.com/watch?v=JnEN2Sm4IIQ.

Students entered the room to the Hawaiian phrase *e komo mai*—"welcome." The classroom was arranged into an archipelago of "islands," each with its own theme and focus, such as grammar, formatting, or transitions. A soft soundtrack of laid-back island music filled the space, turning an ordinary peer review day into an impromptu escape to a tropical retreat. Students hopped from island to island, engaging with peers' writing and providing feedback tailored to each destination's unique customs.

Armed with color-coded pens, students annotated strengths and areas for improvement on each other's work. At regular intervals, they rotated to new islands, leaving behind a visual map of feedback. This iterative process helped students quickly identify patterns and priorities in their writing while reinforcing collaborative learning.

The activity wasn't just about novelty—it mirrored James Paul Gee's concept of affinity spaces, where learners share knowledge and expertise in a community of practice. Thanks to its gamelike design, students embraced their roles, fully engaging with the process while Mathis floated between groups to offer feedback. By the end, students not only improved their writing but gained a deeper appreciation for peer review as a collaborative and iterative process.

AN UNEXPECTED VIDEO PUTS A SMILE ON FIFTH GRADERS' FACES

For Thomas Bussey, a fifth-grade teacher in Atlanta, Georgia, teaching isn't just about delivering material—it's about creating unforgettable experiences. In one inventive lesson, a simple review of sentence revisions transformed into an epic showdown with none other than the Joker, played by Bussey himself in a clever video.

The lesson began with a Powtoon video introducing key concepts. Then the screen glitched and the Joker appeared. Declaring that he had the classroom surrounded, the Clown Prince of Crime taunted the students with his trademark cackle, even singling out one: "I'm coming for you—especially *you*, Hector!" Laughter erupted, and the students were instantly hooked.

What followed was a classroom-wide boss battle. Students became superheroes tasked with defeating the Joker's henchmen. Around the room, prompts guarded by "villains" challenged the students to correct flawed sentences. By collaborating to solve these puzzles, the class worked together to thwart the Joker.

The true genius of this lesson wasn't just its spectacle. By reframing a traditional assessment into a gamelike, collaborative battle, Bussey gave his students a clearer sense of purpose. Each activity fed directly into the larger goal: to defeat the big bad boss. This approach mirrors James Paul Gee's insights into how games create meaningful, immediate feedback and a sense of progression, helping learners connect their actions to a greater objective.

Reflecting on his approach, Bussey said, "My classroom is a place of imagination, challenge, and storytelling. From video surprises to boss battles, our class game motivates my students to achieve more than they ever thought possible." For his students, the lesson was more than fun—it was a purposeful, immersive experience they won't forget. And when students are fully engaged and motivated to give their best effort? That's no joke.

ZOINKS! A COLLEGE CLASSROOM BECOMES A SLEUTH SQUAD

For Dr. Gwendolyn Deger, transforming a special education course syllabus into a Scooby-Doo-themed game manual wasn't just about adding flair—it was about redefining how students engaged with course content.

Presented as Scooby-Doo and the Case of the Excluded Classroom, the gamified syllabus for Dr. Deger's education course at Westminster College in New Wilmington, Pennsylvania, invited students to become members of the Sleuth Squad, embarking on a semester-long mystery adventure.

The gamified course manual flipped the traditional syllabus on its head, introducing self-paced learning quests, themed leader badges, and spooky power-up collectibles. These elements framed the study of the Individuals with Disabilities Education Act and special education principles as a heroic journey. Students accumulated "shards of light," representing knowledge and skills while tackling creative challenges such as writing social stories, building assistive technology showcases, and designing ADA-compliant spaces.

Dr. Deger's playful design aligns deeply with James Paul Gee's concept of affinity spaces—immersive, collaborative environments where learners rally around shared purpose. Her classroom became just that, with students leveraging the Scooby-Doo theme to work as a team while mastering complex content. The novelty of the theme, coupled with the inclusivity of the design, exemplified Gee's assertion that learning thrives when it's active, social, and meaningful.

Reflecting on her approach, Dr. Deger noted, "My students are genuinely intrigued and engaged during class. They're using their textbooks more than ever and diving deeper into concepts I couldn't cover in lecture-based courses. By meeting students where they are, I can encourage them to explore their own interests and how those intersect with our course content. Every day feels like a new adventure."

Through this innovative syllabus, Dr. Deger reminded her students—and the wider educational community—that serious play isn't just for little kids. Whether solving mysteries with Scooby-Doo or addressing real-world challenges in education, her gamified approach proves that thoughtful design can transform classrooms into inspiring spaces of collaboration, curiosity, and growth.

A PLAYBOOK FOR PLAY

A great classroom game, like a flywheel, builds power with every rotation. It doesn't just make learning fun—it creates momentum that reshapes how students approach challenge, collaboration, and creativity. Once students experience a classroom where play and rigor go hand in hand, there's no going back to passive learning. The wheel is in motion. The game is on.

In this chapter's playbook, we're spotlighting a collection of activities that embody the principles of playful pedagogy and gamified learning. These resources have been designed and refined over the years to deliver that same sense of immersive excitement, all without requiring weeks of preparation or instruction. Think of them as your secret weapon—activities that sneak the hard work of learning past students' defenses by disguising it as pure fun.

RESOURCE RUMBLE

Game On
Think of eight different activities your students can complete to show what they know about your current unit of study. These can include listing facts, defining vocab words, or drawing pictures—anything goes! The catch? Each task should be repeatable, with no finite number of "correct" submissions. Get the picture?

Take these eight tasks and stash them in identical envelopes or boxes, each containing exactly one task apiece. Place all the envelopes on a central desk alongside a six-sided die and a bag of building blocks (LEGO works great if you've got them), and you're ready to rumble!

A Playful Upgrade
This is a better way of looking at a review day through a bunch of different lenses at once.

Quick-Start Guide

1. **Divide the class:** Group everyone into teams.
2. **Start a timer:** You can decide how long each round should be.
3. **Select an envelope:** One representative from each team picks an envelope and takes it back to their group to solve.
4. **Spot-check teams:** After completing the task, teams call you over for a quick spot-check to confirm the task meets your standards.
5. **Roll:** If you approve a team's task, they roll the die to determine how many building blocks they add to their tower.
6. **Repeat:** Teams return the envelopes and repeat until time is up. The team with the tallest tower wins!

Pedagogy Power-Up

Look for accuracy, effort, and creativity in students' work. Offer quick feedback to keep the game moving—and feel free to ask clarifying questions on the fly to really compel a team to explain their thinking (while helping to keep the game close and competitive between all teams).

House Rules

Not sure what tasks would work best for your class? Ask AI tools like ChatGPT to help design unique challenges tailored to your curriculum. They could be anything from fact-finding activities to creative writing prompts. Then work with AI to craft a themed backstory for your activity. (Example: "A hurricane is approaching! Can you survive the storm? Work as rival castaway tribes to build the tallest shelter before time runs out!") Once again, a clever bit of theme work makes the dream work!

UDL for the Win

Resource Rumble transforms a simple review session into a dynamic, inclusive learning experience. It engages students with playful competition, supports representation through varied task types and multimodal options, and empowers action and expression by giving all students the chance to contribute in meaningful ways.

- **Engagement** (the *why* of learning): Resource Rumble turns a traditional review day into an exciting, hands-on competition that keeps all students actively involved. The combination of choice, collaboration, and a playful objective—building the tallest tower—sparks joy and intrinsic motivation. Incorporating thematic elements like natural disasters or futuristic adventures heightens curiosity and makes the activity feel fresh and relevant to your curriculum.
- **Representation** (the *what* of learning): With eight different modalities to choose from, students will organically engage with a variety of task types—such as listing facts, defining vocabulary, or drawing visuals—that can be remixed and reimagined in any combination you see fit. Using accessible visuals, clear task prompts, or even different icons to signify the task for each selection further ensures that all students can participate meaningfully.
- **Action and expression** (the *how* of learning): Teams demonstrate their knowledge through iterative play: completing tasks, building towers, and strategizing their next moves. This process allows students to showcase their strengths, whether through problem-solving, creativity, or presentation skills. Sharing final towers in a celebratory showcase fosters pride in their efforts and builds a sense of accomplishment, while teacher feedback on accuracy and creativity deepens understanding.

SAVE OUR STUDENTS

Game On
Dust off your trusty worksheets or graphic organizers and scan them into a single shared slide deck, turning your classroom into a mystery-packed team challenge. Inspired by the hit mobile game *Among Us*, students must work together to complete all tasks in a collaborative deck while identifying sneaky saboteurs before time runs out.

A Playful Upgrade
This replaces ho-hum worksheets with peer review that becomes a class-wide whodunit!

Quick-Start Guide

1. **Create a shared slide deck:** Include eight to ten different activities (e.g., vocab definitions, graphic organizers, Venn diagrams), with a different activity on each slide. Provide an example or two as necessary, but try to leave the activities themselves as blank as possible! Each slide should feature the type of tasks that will take a ton of thinking.
2. **Add a themed background:** Consider adding a spaceship, haunted house, or fantasy castle to the slide template background for even more immersion.
3. **Select saboteurs:** Fire up your favorite tech tool like Remind (or a simple email) to secretly message three to five students about their saboteur roles.
4. **Share the slide deck with your class:** Be sure to give everyone editing privileges at the same time.
5. **Explain the challenge:** The class must complete every slide collaboratively while rooting out the saboteurs trying to derail their work.

6. **Saboteurs secretly edit slides:** While the class plays, saboteurs delay progress by cleverly changing a few things here and there—not by deleting entire submissions outright.
7. **Students vote on suspected saboteurs:** Once outed, saboteurs join the good guys and help complete tasks for the rest of the game.
8. **Calling the win:** The class wins if all tasks are completed *and* all saboteurs are identified. The saboteurs win if any tasks remain incomplete when time runs out.

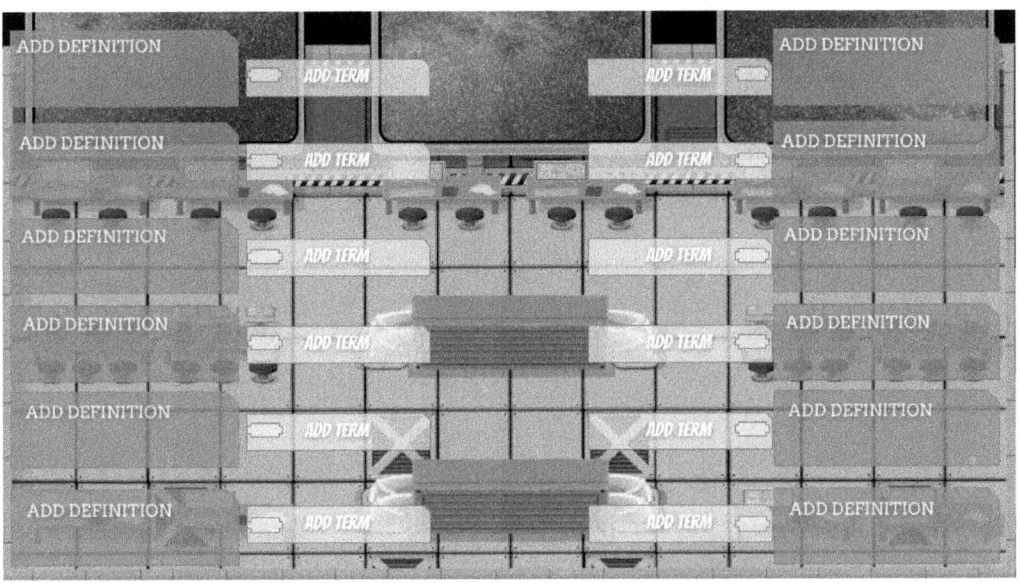

Pedagogy Power-Up

Encourage your student saboteurs to be subtle with their edits, adding small errors or deleting content without drawing attention to themselves. Their classmates are going to have to look extra closely every time the slideshow gets edited! "Columbus sailed the ocean blue in . . . 1493? Hey, wait just a second here . . ."

House Rules

Use AI tools like ChatGPT to craft a themed opening script for your game. (Example: "Welcome aboard the spaceship! Your mission is to repair critical systems before oxygen runs out. But beware: Traitors are among you!") Use Google Slides' revision history to recap all the excitement as a class when your game ends (but let students know that this feature is off-limits during gameplay).

UDL for the Win

Save Our Students combines collaborative problem-solving with a thrilling mystery game that keeps students on the edge of their seats. It engages learners with an immersive, high-stakes challenge, supports representation through diverse task types and accessible visuals, and empowers action and expression by encouraging every student to contribute to the group's success.

- **Engagement** (the *why* of learning): The fast-paced, mystery-solving nature of the activity grabs students' attention and builds excitement. Adding thematic elements, such as a spaceship in distress or a haunted house, immerses students in the story and keeps them emotionally invested. Working against the clock fosters urgency, teamwork, and focus, ensuring that every student is actively engaged.
- **Representation** (the *what* of learning): The variety of tasks on each new slide—ranging from vocabulary definitions to diagram completions—offers multiple pathways for students to engage with the content and interact with their teammates. By incorporating consistent visual aids, thematic backgrounds, and simple prompts in the shared slide deck, the activity ensures accessibility for diverse learners while the cooperative element gives students the chance to peer review and learn from their classmates in real time! Saboteur roles introduce an

additional layer of challenge for students who thrive on strategy and creativity.
- **Action and expression** (the *how* of learning): Students collaborate to complete tasks, solve puzzles, and identify saboteurs, offering multiple ways to demonstrate their understanding. This activity encourages critical thinking, teamwork, and decision-making, allowing students to shine in different roles, whether as problem solvers, editors, or detectives. And to top it all off, introducing that clever little monkey wrench of trying to work together while sussing out the saboteurs adds a reflective element that reinforces communication and analytical skills at every step along the way.

COLLAB COLLECT

Game On
You don't need to teach a STEM class to bring an exciting engineering twist to your lessons. Collab Collect is a perfect icebreaker or a content-driven challenge that works any time of year. Whether your goal is fostering teamwork, sparking creativity, or reinforcing curriculum concepts, this quick, simple, and endlessly adaptable activity will quickly become a staple in your teacher tool kit.

A Playful Upgrade
Infuse traditional STEM activities with on-the-fly problem-solving, strategy, and team-based collaboration.

Quick-Start Guide

1. **Set the challenge:** Divide students into small teams and present them with a STEM challenge of your choice, such as:
    a. Build a bridge: Construct a bridge to span a gap of [x] inches.
    b. Tower of power: Build a tower at least [y] inches tall.

2. **Include the Twist:** Teams begin the challenge with no materials. The only way to earn supplies is by collaborating to identify things they have in common. For every set of five shared connections they list, they gain one material to use in their project.
3. **Build and earn:** Supply teams with basic construction materials (e.g., index cards, tape, paper, popsicle sticks) to choose from at a central hub. As they list more connections, they can continue earning additional items to enhance their design.
4. **Time it:** Set a timer to keep the energy up and encourage quick thinking. Once time runs out, measure and test their creations to celebrate successes.

Pedagogy Power-Up

After the activity, reflect on the importance of collaboration. What strategies did teams use to find common ground? How did communication impact their success? Adapt the materials or challenge goals to align with your curriculum and revisit this activity throughout the year.

House Rules

Supercharge this activity with AI! Use tools like ChatGPT to generate quick lists of STEM challenges or suggest creative materials for construction using whatever supplies you happen to have lying around. Want to make it even more thematic? Ask AI to craft a storyline or scenario, like "build a shelter to survive a desert island," and share these results as part of your activity rollout to heighten engagement all the more.

UDL for the Win

Collab Collect combines engineering challenges with creative collaboration, making it a perfect activity for fostering teamwork and critical thinking. It engages students with the excitement of earning materials, supports representation through diverse methods of participation, and empowers action and expression by encouraging students to solve problems in innovative ways.

- **Engagement** (the *why* of learning): This activity keeps students actively involved by transforming teamwork into a gamified challenge. The thrill of uncovering connections to earn supplies motivates students to communicate and collaborate. Adding a storyline, like building a survival shelter or designing a futuristic tower, ups the stakes and immerses students in a creative scenario, making the task feel relevant and exciting.
- **Representation** (the *what* of learning): This activity ensures all sorts of accessibility by presenting information and tasks in diverse, multimodal formats. Clear task prompts can be paired with visuals or icons, making it easier for students to understand what's required. For example, you could provide a visual

checklist of connections made or a chart to track earned materials. Thematic elements, like building a bridge over lava or constructing a tower on Mars, provide a narrative context that supports comprehension by grounding the activity in relatable, imaginative scenarios. Using a variety of materials and examples ensures that all students can process the activity in ways that align with their individual needs and strengths.

- **Action and expression** (the *how* of learning): This hands-on challenge gives students the chance to problem-solve, test their designs, and refine their approaches as a team. Whether brainstorming connections, strategizing their builds, or presenting their final creations, every student has a role to play. The scalable complexity of the task ensures all learners can contribute meaningfully while giving advanced students opportunities to stretch their creativity and engineering skills. Reflecting on the process afterward reinforces communication and teamwork, helping students grow as collaborators and problem solvers.

QUESTIONS FOR DISCUSSION

1. How can educators strike the right balance between novelty and rigor when integrating gamification into their classrooms? Drawing from examples like Kathleen Mathis's Peer Review Paradise and Thomas Bussey's Joker-themed lesson, what principles can guide the design of activities that both engage and deepen learning?

2. James Paul Gee's concept of affinity spaces emphasizes the power of shared purpose and collaboration. How might activities like Dr. Gwendolyn Deger's Scooby-Doo-themed syllabus or the collaborative Save Our Students challenge foster these spaces? What strategies could you use to ensure every learner feels included and valued within these playful environments?

3. Mihaly Csikszentmihalyi's flow theory highlights the importance of matching challenges to skill levels. Reflect on the activities presented in this chapter. How do they help students enter a state of flow? What adjustments could you make to your own lessons to ensure learners experience deep focus, engagement, and intrinsic motivation?

I HOPE YOU LIVE A LIFE YOU'RE PROUD OF, AND IF YOU FIND THAT YOU'RE NOT, I HOPE YOU HAVE THE STRENGTH TO START ALL OVER AGAIN.

— F. SCOTT FITZGERALD —

CHAPTER 5

EMPOWER THEIR CHOICES

VOICE, AUTONOMY, AND MOTIVATION

Hey, gang. John here again.

Back in chapter 3, I mentioned how I broke my foot—an injury that knocked me flat and sidelined me for months. What I didn't share then was just how humbling the recovery process turned out to be.

Funnily enough, the break wasn't the result of anything outrageous, risky, or reckless. And as much as I wish I could say, "You should see the other guy," I can't.

Nope. It was a freak accident.

Picture this: It's a beautiful, sunny afternoon on the longest day of the year. There's a friendly church league softball game on the National Mall in Washington, DC. My team—a bunch of spirited but athletically suspect thirty- and forty-somethings—was already getting steamrolled. Zero chance of winning.

Late in the seventh inning, down by more than a dozen runs, I planted my foot *just the wrong way* while trying to field a very slow-rolling ground ball.

Bang. That was all she wrote.

Your humble narrator: 0. Father Time: 1.

Now, don't get me wrong. I know this sort of thing could happen to anybody. But I've always considered myself in pretty decent shape. I eat right, sleep well, and—thanks to good enough genes and just questionable enough common sense—I've run more than three dozen marathons, half marathons, and harebrained endurance races over the last decade.

So, yeah. The injury caught me off guard. But what really floored me was the recovery.

The break left me with a nasty surgical scar, and behind it was the steel plate that was bolted into my bone. Months on crutches brought radiating pain, muscle atrophy, and about twenty pounds of extra weight. By the time my doctors looked at removing all the hardware, they found some pretty serious nerve damage.

Their verdict? It would be in my best interest never to run long distances again.

When you're staring down a setback, it's easy to feel powerless. The mountain of what you can't do feels insurmountable. But no one tells you this: You always have a choice. Always.

I didn't get to choose the injury. I didn't get to choose the doctor's timeline. But I *did* get to choose what happened next. And those choices—tiny as they seemed—were everything.

Would I focus on what I couldn't do or celebrate the inch of progress I could make each day? Would I take the small steps—tedious stretches, endless ice packs, stubborn attempts at walking without a limp—over and over until I clawed my way back?

I chose not to run away from the challenge but to lean into a new one. I joined a CrossFit gym.

Did I know the first thing about CrossFit? Nope. Had I ever lifted weights before? Not even close. But here's the thing: I needed to choose to do *something*. And the beauty of choice is that small choices become big choices. Momentum builds. One step becomes two. Two become ten. Before you know it, you're not just recovering—you're redefining what's possible.

And this is every bit as true for classrooms as it is for broken bones.

The key to growth is choice. When we give students meaningful opportunities to make decisions in their learning, they're not just passive pawns in someone else's game; they become active players, strategizing their next moves. Those small choices—what to explore, how to express themselves, how to tackle challenges—become the foundation for bigger decisions that shape their journey.

In our classrooms (just like in our workout regimens), real growth happens when learners feel like they're the ones steering the ship. When we gamify learning with points, levels, and feedback loops, we're not just making things more fun. We're creating systems that honor choice, celebrate progress, and build purpose. Toss in a few well-placed tech tools that personalize those challenges? Suddenly, your students are no longer passengers. They're players. And they're firmly in control of the game.

In this chapter, we'll take a closer look at what happens when we design learning experiences that honor the incredible power of student choice. Because the getback is always greater than the setback. And it all starts with one small, meaningful decision.

STRONGER EVERY DAY

Not everyone's a CrossFit junkie, and that's okay. But there's something undeniably compelling about what happens inside those stripped-down, garage-style gyms. No fancy machines. No oversized mirrors. Just people pushing themselves, one rep, one yes, one choice, one breakthrough at a time. It's oddly romantic. Almost Rocky Balboa-esque, even.

And that's the power of the approach: it's all voluntary. No one's forcing you to show up, let alone to lift heavier, move faster, or try something new. Each day presents a new array of options and obstacles. And every bit of progress starts with a choice, a decision to step into something hard—not because you have to but because you're ready for a challenge, and you're choosing to grow.

And the real "Eye of the Tiger"? It's not just in the workouts. It's in the mindset. CrossFit's founder, Greg Glassman, once described the program's goal like this: "We sought to build a program that would best prepare trainees for any physical contingency—prepare them not only for the unknown but for the unknowable as well."

Now let's take that same sentiment and apply it to the classroom, where the stakes might just be even higher: "We sought to build a program that would best prepare *students* for any *mental* contingency—prepare them not only for the unknown but for the unknowable as well."

Imagine treating our classrooms like mental gymnasiums, using the curriculum as core exercises to build grit, resilience, and brain muscle. Training students to be so strong and sure of their abilities that they're ready for whatever challenges life throws their way.

Actually, that does sound kinda badass, don't you think? Because when we help students grow stronger, we're not just preparing them for tests; we're preparing them for life. Isn't that the real end game of everything that we do as educators?

The pros are inclined to agree.

Let's step out of the gym and back into the classroom for a moment. As it happens, researchers have been exploring this idea from a cognitive angle for decades. So let's turn our attention to the brilliant work of Elizabeth Ligon Bjork and her husband, Robert Bjork, two renowned psychology professors at UCLA. This powerhouse duo has spent decades studying how we learn best, and in 2011, they introduced the concept of desirable difficulties—a framework that flips the script. According to their research, the best learning doesn't come from ease and comfort; it comes from the right kind of struggle.

Wait a minute—*desirable* difficulties?

Absolutely.

As the Bjorks put it, "Many difficulties are *undesirable* during instruction and forever after. [But] *desirable* difficulties, versus the array of undesirable difficulties, are desirable because they trigger encoding and retrieval processes that support learning, comprehension, and remembering."[25]

The beauty of desirable difficulties is how universal they are, offering strategies that apply to learners of all ages and subjects. Take spaced repetition, for example—it works like building physical strength. Consistent effort, spread out over time, delivers lasting results. Interleaving topics trains the mind to stay agile, much like CrossFit's constantly varied workouts keep athletes ready for anything. And once again, we're talking about choice—giving students the chance to actively engage with their learning through thoughtful, intentional challenges.

If we do it right, struggle is not the enemy of learning; it's the secret ingredient to growth. And the Bjorks' studies show that the best way to build lasting knowledge is to embrace challenges that feel hard in the moment but yield stronger mental "muscle" over time.

Techniques like spacing out study sessions, interleaving topics, and practicing retrieval (like through quizzes or self-testing) might feel frustrating or counterintuitive compared with easier methods like buzzer-style review games or cramming the night before the test. But

---

25 E. L. Bjork and R. A. Bjork, "Making Things Hard on Yourself, but in a Good Way: Creating Desirable Difficulties to Enhance Learning," in *Psychology and the Real World: Essays Illustrating Fundamental Contributions to Society*, eds. M. A. Gernsbacher, R. W. Pew, L. M. Hough, and J. R. Pomerantz (Worth Publishers, 2011): 56–64.

while the latter might provide a fleeting sense of mastery (we're looking at you, Fun Friday and Kahoot!), the Bjorks' work demonstrates that true understanding comes from grappling with the material in ways that force your brain to work just a little bit harder. In other words, learning that feels easy often doesn't stick—but learning that challenges you will.

The takeaway for teachers? Struggle is a feature, not a bug, of meaningful learning. By designing classrooms that encourage effort, reward choice, and teach resilience, we prepare students not only to master today's curriculum but also to tackle the unknowable challenges of the future with confidence and skill.

STUDENTS DESERVE MORE THAN EASY

Some CrossFit gyms use a deceptively simple system that makes the whole experience feel more like leveling up in a video game than grinding through a workout. It's called the Level Method, and it's a color-coded framework that breaks fitness into fifteen distinct categories, from squat endurance to running speed. Like a martial arts belt system, this framework for self-assessment shows exactly where you're thriving and where you still have room to grow. In a lot of ways, it's a real-world example of gamification done right.

And here's what makes it brilliant: Progress is personal. There's no one-size-fits-all score. Instead of chasing perfection, athletes make small, strategic choices—pushing where it matters most and adjusting where they need support.

Sound familiar? It's the same core idea behind standards-based grading (SBG), a system designed to break academic progress into clear, measurable components. But while SBG often assesses proficiency in broad subject areas, the Level Method's granular approach goes even further. It tracks performance across multiple domains, delivers real-time feedback, and helps athletes tailor their effort based on individual strengths and needs.

That means every workout becomes a chance to train with purpose. Daily sessions might be preset, but the path through them is up to you. Tackling an "as many reps as possible" (AMRAP) circuit with box jumps, running, and dumbbell presses? You might opt for a twenty-inch box instead of twenty-four, scale the dumbbell weight to match your level, or extend the run to play to a strength. Every choice is intentional, every challenge is scalable, and every decision is driven by self-awareness.

That's the power of intentional challenge. Small adjustments, made by the learner, transform a tough workout into a personalized training ground.

And here's the kicker: Your overall score isn't based on your average. It's based on your two lowest scores. Progress isn't about coasting on your strengths but about confronting your weaknesses head on. That kind of data-driven, growth-focused design avoids the trap of inflated averages masking real learning gaps.

In many ways, it's SBG taken to the next level—gamified, personalized, and powered by student choice.

For educators, the takeaway is clear. If we want students to grow stronger, we need to create classroom "workouts" where they're invited to make meaningful choices, track their own growth, and tackle desirable difficulties one step at a time. Progress, after all, doesn't begin with perfection. It begins with one intentional choice at a time.

Ready to try it for yourself? Here's a reflection activity inspired by the Level Method to help you bring this philosophy into practice.

TEACHER REFLECTION MATRIX: THE RULE OF TWO

Just like in fitness, where we grow strongest by focusing on areas for improvement, effective teaching requires us to identify and address our weakest spots. Inspired by the Level Method, this activity will help you reflect on your current strengths and pinpoint where you stand to grow.

CLASSROOM MANAGEMENT	WHITE	YELLOW	ORANGE	BLUE	PURPLE	BROWN	BLACK
CURRICULAR KNOWLEDGE	WHITE	YELLOW	ORANGE	BLUE	PURPLE	BROWN	BLACK
LESSON PLANNING	WHITE	YELLOW	ORANGE	BLUE	PURPLE	BROWN	BLACK
FAMILY COMMUNICATION	WHITE	YELLOW	ORANGE	BLUE	PURPLE	BROWN	BLACK
INNOVATIVE TEACHING	WHITE	YELLOW	ORANGE	BLUE	PURPLE	BROWN	BLACK
TECHNOLOGY INTEGRATION	WHITE	YELLOW	ORANGE	BLUE	PURPLE	BROWN	BLACK
TIMELY FEEDBACK	WHITE	YELLOW	ORANGE	BLUE	PURPLE	BROWN	BLACK
ESTABLISHING RAPPORT	WHITE	YELLOW	ORANGE	BLUE	PURPLE	BROWN	BLACK
EXTRACURRICULAR SUPPORT	WHITE	YELLOW	ORANGE	BLUE	PURPLE	BROWN	BLACK
INFLUENCING COLLEAGUES	WHITE	YELLOW	ORANGE	BLUE	PURPLE	BROWN	BLACK

Step 1: Assess Your Baseline

Rate yourself across ten teaching indicators on a scale from 1 (beginner/white) to 7 (elite/black), using only whole numbers. Don't worry about sharing your scores with any colleagues—this exercise is merely a chance for you to dig a little deeper into your own personal goals and performance standards based on whatever criteria you feel comfortable using. Here are the indicators for this self-assessment:

- Classroom management
- Curricular knowledge
- Lesson planning
- Family communication
- Innovative teaching
- Technology integration
- Timely feedback
- Establishing rapport
- Extracurricular support
- Influencing colleagues

Be honest! And remember that this is a baseline, not a final score.

Step 2: Apply the Rule of Two

Don't just take the average score of every one of your results. Instead, take the average of your two *lowest* scores. Got it? These areas will become your focus points for growth—the desired difficulty that will challenge you most, but ultimately yield the most meaningful progress.

Why focus on your weakest spots?

Just as athletes don't grow stronger by coasting, learners thrive when we engage with challenges that stretch us. Sure, we can all bust out a quick max-effort bench press for a single rep and then spend the rest of the day taking selfies and flexing our vanity muscles while we down the teacher equivalent of protein shakes. But is that really what we got into this profession for? By honing your skills where you feel least comfortable, you'll be primed to make the most real, transformative gains in every area of your professional practice.

Step 3: Set Your Action Plan

Do the following for each of your two lowest categories:

1. Identify one concrete action step you can take this month to address the area.
   Example: If family communication was a low score, you might set a goal to send personalized emails or updates to all families twice per month.
2. Consider how you can involve your strengths to improve these areas.
   Example: If technology integration is a strength, think about how you might be able to leverage AI tools to improve timely feedback or lesson planning.

Step 4: Reflect and Repeat

At the end of the month, reassess yourself on the same matrix. Note where you've improved and identify any lingering challenges. Repeat the Rule of Two strategy regularly to keep your focus clear, actionable, and growth driven.

Remember: This method isn't about perfection—it's about progress. By targeting areas for growth while celebrating your strengths, you'll build a sustainable path to becoming the most effective, reflective version of yourself as an educator.

Much like the Level Method transforms workouts into targeted growth journeys, this approach to teaching helps you embrace desired difficulties and grow stronger where it matters most. And just like in fitness, choices are transformational. It's the effort you put in that makes all the difference.

GET YOUR STUDENTS IN THE GAME

We've talked about identifying your own growth areas as educators, so now let's bring that powerful mindset into the classroom. Because the truth is that students deserve the same clarity and opportunity to recognize *their* progress. When we equip students with meaningful ways to track their growth and push through their own desired difficulties, we're not just helping them succeed in school—we're teaching them to embrace a growth mindset for life.

So here's the challenge: Let's explore how you can design a Level Method–style system for your students. And we're going to use a little AI-powered brainstorming magic to make it happen.

Step 1: Select Your Indicators

Start by identifying the core skills or categories in your content area where students can grow and show progress. Think of these as the muscle groups of your classroom—foundational skills that students need to build over time. If you're working in an SBG environment, these categories might already be a part of your existing playbook, but feel free to tweak, tinker, and add any additional items of your own. For example:

- **ELA:** Reading comprehension, writing structure, vocabulary development, presentation skills, research quality
- **Math:** Problem-solving, fluency with equations, conceptual understanding, speed and accuracy, group collaboration
- **Science:** Lab work, scientific writing, hypothesis testing, data analysis, research presentations
- **Social studies:** Historical analysis, argument building, source evaluation, map reading, debate skills

Pro tip: Not sure where to start? Fire up ChatGPT as your brainstorming partner. Feed it a quick prompt like "I'm teaching [subject/grade]. What are eight to ten indicators that would help students track their progress in [specific skills] over time?" Let the AI help you generate ideas quickly and customize them to match your content standards.

Step 2: Set the Baseline

Once you've got your list of indicators, it's time for students to assess their starting point. Introduce the concept of the baseline assessment and have students rate themselves on a scale. Use something simple like 1 (beginner) to 7 (proficient). Remind them this is *not a grade* but a tool for growth.

Step 3: Apply the Rule of Two

Once again, here's where it gets real. Rather than average all their scores, students focus on their two lowest indicators—the areas that challenge them the most. These are their personalized growth zones, where small steps will lead to the biggest gains.

From an educator's perspective, the Rule of Two is a classic UDL-aligned strategy, offering students multiple means of action and expression by customizing their challenge level. Instead of a one-size-fits-all task, students identify their own growth zones and set personalized targets. Just like a well-designed classroom assessment, the Rule of Two ensures that struggle isn't arbitrary or overwhelming—it's productive. By letting students focus their energy where it's needed most, we empower them to actively shape their learning journey achieve the growth they're looking for.

Step 4: Create Action Steps

For each low-score category, students set one concrete, achievable action step to improve. For example:

- If "Research quality" is low, a student might plan to use one new source type (like a primary source) in their next project.
- If "Vocabulary development" needs work, a student could focus on learning five new content-specific words that week.

Encourage students to revisit these indicators regularly (weekly or monthly) and track their gains. Celebrate every bit of growth—because progress is the goal.

When students see a clear road map of where they are *and* where they can go, the mountain of learning doesn't feel so intimidating. Their choices make it clear that they're always in control of their progress. They're not just showing up; they're leveling up.

And you? You're guiding them through targeted, meaningful challenges while giving them plenty of choices and all kinds of ownership of their learning. It's the perfect blend of growth mindset, gamification, and desired difficulty—all powered by student choice.

Just like CrossFitters track their progress in the gym, your students can build their own mental muscle in the classroom. With clear indicators, actionable goals, and a little AI support to get you started, you've got everything you need to help your students embrace challenges, celebrate progress, and grow stronger every day.

A PLAYBOOK FOR CHOICE

It's time to move from theory to action. If there's one thing we've learned so far, it's that some degree of real, meaningful choice isn't just a nicety in education—it's a necessity. Whether it's recovering from a setback, building grit, or leveling up our skills, choice puts us in the driver's seat so we can take ownership of our growth. And the same holds true for our students.

But designing opportunities for choice in the classroom doesn't mean handing over the keys to an empty mental gymnasium and saying, "Go figure it out." As James Clear, author of *Atomic Habits*, once succinctly noted: "You do not rise to the level of your goals. You fall to the level of your systems." Just like in CrossFit or the Level Method, the most impactful progress happens when we combine freedom with structure, providing clear, actionable pathways that guide students toward success while allowing them to customize their journey.

In our classrooms, this can take many different forms. Here are just a few we like to keep in mind when we help teachers envision the sorts of mental gymnasiums they can create.

Choose Your Core Exercises

Just like athletes rely on foundational movements like squats or push-ups to build strength, students need core exercises that anchor their learning. In the parlance of UDL, this is all about action and expression. Think of these as the nonnegotiables in your curriculum—essential skills like critical reading, problem-solving, or writing structure. Providing choice here means letting students decide *how* to demonstrate mastery: an essay, storyboard, podcast, or video presentation. The content stays consistent, but the path to mastery is flexible.

Need a hand setting up your ideal layout? Lean on AI tools for suggestions that can help provide your learners with just the right blend of desired difficulty and appeal.

Choose Your Difficulty

In fitness, scaling a workout allows athletes to tackle challenges at their level. The same holds true in the classroom. Give students opportunities to strategically adjust the difficulty of a task while still meeting learning goals. Offer tiered assignments, optional challenge problems, or level-up extensions for those ready to push harder. This empowers students to step outside their comfort zones without feeling overwhelmed or under-challenged.

Choose Your Strategy

Whether you're tackling a workout or a tough project, the right strategy makes all the difference. In the classroom, this could mean allowing students to decide *how* they approach a task—work solo, collaborate in pairs, or split responsibilities as a team. It might also remind you that there are all sorts of ways to deliver content to your students, like instructional videos, podcasts, or peer-to-peer conversations. It doesn't have to be traditional long-form lectures or teacher-guided presentations. In the world of UDL, this is all about representation and giving learners multiple means of access to the same material. By giving them agency over their strategy, you build decision-making skills while reinforcing that success is about finding the approach that works best for them.

Choose Your Partners

CrossFitters often train with partners who push them to improve. In your classroom, choice in partnerships can supercharge collaboration. This is a surefire way to spark all sorts of engagement in any classroom (a UDL must-have). Let students decide who they work with during group tasks, or keep things interesting by challenging them to rotate roles within their groups and pair up with additional partners at select intervals throughout the activity. Whether they're strengthening existing relationships or branching out to work with new peers, students learn that teamwork—and intentional choice—can be a huge driver for growth. Look for opportunities to have students tackle certain obstacles as a team.

Choose Your Surprises

Sometimes, the most memorable workouts come with an unexpected twist—like a bonus challenge or a sudden time limit. And creating an environment where your students learn to expect the unexpected is a fantastic way to keep everyone alert and engaged at every turn. Build in small wild cards or creative curveballs like a pop-up debate during a lesson, a mystery task that connects two topics, or a hidden bonus-point system that rewards especially creative thinking. The element of surprise turns routine tasks into energizing opportunities for growth.

By strategically combining these elements (core exercises, difficulty, strategy, partners, and surprises), you'll create dynamic learning experiences where students feel empowered to push themselves. Choice becomes more than a perk; it's the engine that drives curiosity, effort, and progress.

It's time to give your students the power to choose, the tools to thrive, and the confidence to take on whatever challenges come their way. After all, small choices become big choices. And the best learning happens when students feel like they're in control of the game.

Ready to level up? Let's dive in.

DOUBLE-BUBBLE BALANCING ACT

Game On

Introduce your students to the Double-Bubble Balancing Act—a lively and visual twist on a classic compare-and-contrast activity. Double-bubble thinking maps help students organize similarities and differences between two concepts, but in this version, it's all about balance and strategy. Teams must add as many bubbles as they can while ensuring each *difference* has a perfectly matched *counterpoint* on the other side of the diagram. And for each new branch you add on one side of the diagram, you'll need to add something that is equivalent in type on the other. It's a hilarious mental workout that will have students analyzing, debating, and creatively balancing ideas in real time.

A Playful Upgrade

This enhances traditional compare-and-contrast exercises, tasking students with flexing their creative thinking skills to keep concepts perfectly balanced!

Quick-Start Guide

1. **Set the stage:** Introduce two seemingly unrelated concepts (e.g., tacos and burgers or clouds and cotton candy). The sillier the pairing, the better!
2. **Build the chart:** Students (or teams) create their charts on paper, on a whiteboard, or with digital tools. For every *similarity* they identify, they get to add a new bubble in the center area between these two items. However, for every *difference* they list, they must provide an equal counterpoint to keep the diagram balanced. Example: "Tacos have shells; burgers have buns."
3. **Add pressure:** Time each round for added intensity and circulate between teams to coach them as they build out their diagrams. Challenge teams to expand their charts as much as possible, but remind them that they'll score no points for any remaining imbalanced items (i.e., a difference without a counterpoint).
4. **Give a judge's bonus:** Award extra points to the team that comes up with the most creative or unexpected connections.

Pedagogy Power-Up

Float freely between groups as they work to offer on-the-fly coaching that prompts them to think critically and creatively as they balance their charts. Ask probing questions to deepen understanding: "Why does this belong on one side?" or "Can you think of a broader similarity?" Channel your favorite CrossFit coach and offer on-the-spot feedback to guide teams toward more nuanced and thoughtful comparisons. This not only keeps the game competitive but also reinforces higher-order thinking.

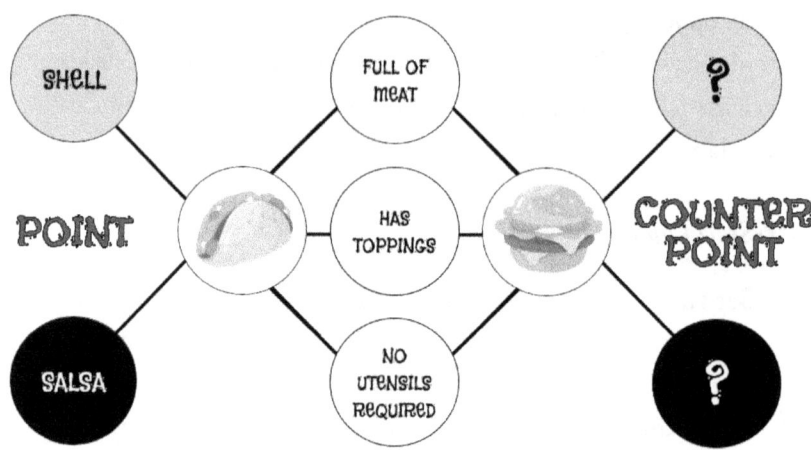

House Rules

- **Thematic twist:** Adapt the activity for any subject or content area! Compare historical figures (e.g., George Washington vs. Abraham Lincoln), scientific terms (e.g., mammals vs. reptiles), or literary concepts (e.g., fiction vs. nonfiction). But throw the ordinary out the window as you mix and match the most unlikely of balancing act prompts by pairing something from your content area (e.g., Lady Macbeth) with something that's completely off the wall and right up your students' alley (e.g., Sydney Sweeney).
- **More space:** Provide your students with oversized sheets of chart paper to give them even more real estate to build out their Double-Bubble Balancing Acts. And if they exceed the space available on the chart paper? Encourage them to keep adding information using sticky notes or full-size pieces of printer paper. The bigger, the better!

- **Digital adaptation:** Use collaborative tools like Google Slides or Padlet so teams can build their charts in real time.
- **AI assist:** For advanced play, let teams use AI tools like ChatGPT to generate wild-card prompts that add a new layer to the comparison. Example prompt: "What's something tacos and burgers have in common that most people wouldn't expect?"

UDL for the Win

Double-Bubble Balancing Act is perfect for diverse learners, blending visual, verbal, and logical thinking with collaborative problem-solving.

- **Engagement** (the *why* of learning): This activity transforms a routine exercise into an interactive competition, making learning joyful and purposeful. The playful element of balance encourages students to stay engaged, while unexpected comparisons spark curiosity and creativity.
- **Representation** (the *what* of learning): By using a variety of modalities—visual diagrams, written explanations, and group discussions—students engage with content in multiple ways. Provide starter ideas, sentence stems, or visual aids for accessibility, ensuring everyone can participate meaningfully.
- **Action and expression** (the *how* of learning): Students showcase their understanding through iterative play, building and revising their charts collaboratively. The balancing act encourages strategic thinking and highlights individual strengths, while the final showcase celebrates effort and achievement.

PYRAMID PASS AND DASH

Game On

Think of this as a mental AMRAP ("as many reps as possible"), but instead of burpees or squats, students are racing against the clock to climb up and down a series of pyramids, completing different mental exercises at each level.

A Challenging Upgrade

This improves on the traditional content recap. Suddenly, "show what you know" becomes a gamified AMRAP for team-based learning.

Quick-Start Guide

1. **Build the pyramids:** On your whiteboard, draw a series of pyramid shapes in rows with dots along the side to indicate their height (e.g., two dots = two tasks, three dots = three tasks, etc.). Each pyramid represents an escalating challenge.
2. **Create your exercise bank:** Provide a bank of available mental exercises that align with your content. Your students will choose from these to make their way through this obstacle course. Here are some sample tasks:
   - Define a key vocab term from this unit
   - Sketch a visual summary
   - Write a HOT (higher-order thinking) question
   - Write a one-sentence summary
   - Create a mnemonic device
   - Draft an analogy
3. **Climb the pyramids:** Students work in teams to complete the challenges step by step. Each step up the pyramid requires a new output style—but there are no repeats allowed until they make it to the top of a pyramid! For instance, students might write two analogies at step 1, sketch three visual summaries at step 2, and so on. When the team reaches the top, they must work back down by tackling these tasks again in reverse order.
4. **Rotate the artisan role:** Only one student (designated as the artisan) can write, draw, or physically build for their team during each step of play, while their teammates offer coaching, strategy,

and ideas. Rotate the artisan role for every step up or down the pyramid.

Pedagogy Power-Up

Reflect on how the rotation of the artisan role impacted teamwork. What strategies helped teams maximize each member's strengths? Encourage students to discuss how collaboration and creative problem-solving contributed to their success and how to adapt future tasks to emphasize skills they wish to develop further.

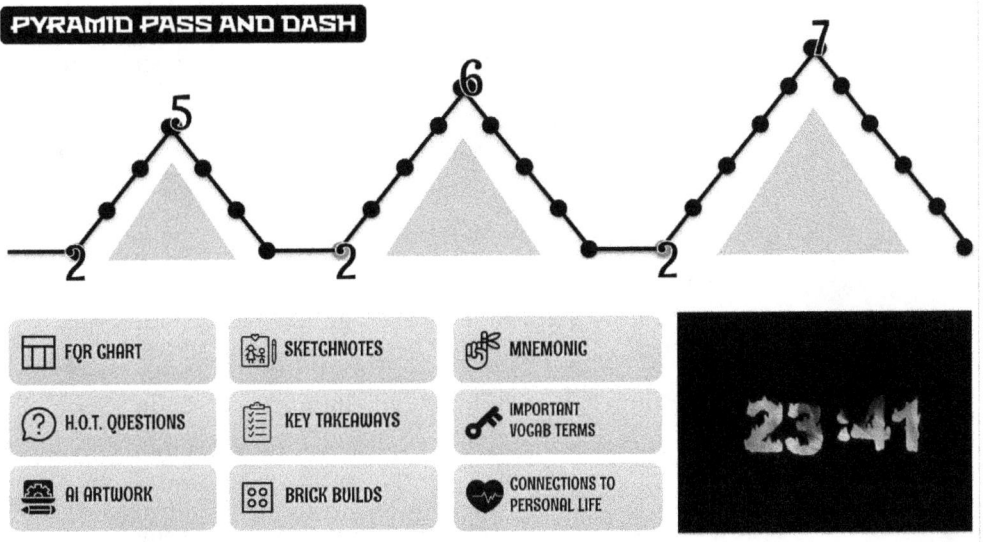

House Rules

- **Add a timer:** This increases the urgency and the fun! A classic AMRAP format means teams are racing to finish as many pyramids as possible before time runs out—but encourage students to compete against their own personal bests, not against the scores of their classmates.

- **Encourage creativity and variety:** Let students pitch their own mental exercises or use AI tools like ChatGPT to generate fresh challenges tailored to your content area. (Example prompt: "Give me five creative ways to review the causes of the American Revolution.")
- **Add a wild-card round:** For an added twist, have teams complete one teacher-selected challenge for bonus points.

UDL for the Win

Pyramid Pass and Dash empowers students with multiple ways to demonstrate their learning, promoting equity and engagement.

- **Engagement** (the *why* of learning): The gamified structure keeps energy high and students motivated. The rotation of roles ensures everyone contributes meaningfully, while the optional timer can add a sense of urgency. Incorporating themes or storytelling elevates the activity, sparking curiosity and making things feel fresh and exciting.
- **Representation** (the *what* of learning): The varied task types (writing, sketching, building) cater to diverse learning styles. Starter prompts or scaffolds (e.g., sentence stems or visual examples) ensure accessibility, while the artisan rotation gives every student a chance to shine.
- **Action and expression** (the *how* of learning): Through iterative play, students showcase their knowledge and creativity in multiple modalities. The climb-and-descend format fosters collaboration, strategic thinking, and resilience. A celebratory showcase of completed pyramids adds a sense of accomplishment and pride, reinforcing the learning process.

TWELVE-TOPIC STITCH-UP

Game On
Concept mapping is an incredible tool for helping students visualize connections between ideas. In this gamified twist, teams work collaboratively to connect concepts while racing to earn attempts at a high-energy, hands-on challenge inspired by the classic Operation board game. Don't have an Operation board? No problem! The game can easily be adapted as a point-scoring activity where successful connections earn the team bragging rights instead of extractions—though the game board adds a whole new level of fun and excitement that's so worth it.

A Challenging Upgrade
This enhances traditional concept mapping by having teams stitch together connections and test their nerves at the operating table!

Quick-Start Guide

1. **Set the stage:** A concept map typically begins with one central topic and branches out as students link it to related ideas. For this activity, draw a big old circle on your whiteboard with a series of numbered locations around the outside (like the face of a clock). Provide students with blank sheets of paper where they can visually connect their ideas. You can scale up or down the number of items (e.g., a ten-topic map, an eight-topic map) to meet class needs.
2. **Chart your connections:** Write the name of exactly one concept from your current unit of study at each numbered location on your diagram. Students choose any *one* concept to begin with and must work as a team to identify connections between that topic and any *five* others. Connections must be written clearly, explaining how the two concepts relate. Keep in mind that every team is working independently of the others! So there's no time spent

on the bench waiting to take your turn while another team plays the game.

3. **Operate:** Once a team successfully maps five connections, they call you over to spot-check what they've done. If the connections are up to snuff by your standards, the team sends a "surgeon" to the Operation board to attempt extracting a piece. A steady hand and nerves of steel are required. If the board buzzes, the item stays, and the team must map out five *new* connections to earn another shot.

4. **Keep the energy up:** Whether they succeeded or failed in the extraction, teams return the piece to the Operation board for other teams to play with. Then they return to their home desk groups to continue concept mapping while other teams take their extraction turn, keeping gameplay in a perpetual state of flow with minimal interruptions. The team with the most successful extractions (or connections, if you're skipping the Operation board) wins when time runs out.

Pedagogy Power-Up

This activity, with its gamified twist, fits seamlessly into classroom review. Students love the high-energy thrill of connecting ideas, and the tactile fun of the Operation board (or a point system) adds just the right dose of suspense. When the game's over, the concept maps themselves double as visual study guides—just snap a photo or hang them up as colorful classroom decor for an instant, content-rich display. Reset your materials, and you're all set for another round whenever inspiration strikes!

House Rules

Want to add even more challenge? Throw in a few random concepts that have absolutely nothing to do with your current unit of study (e.g., a middle school geometry class suddenly has to find five things that the Pythagorean theorem has in common with . . . Kansas City Chiefs quarterback Patrick Mahomes?), and don't be afraid to put your foot on the scale, so to speak. You can slow individual teams down as they work by requiring bonus explanations for any connections that you feel are especially tricky. No board? No problem. Assign creative themes to earn points. Connections could be stitched up with a focus on historical events, scientific processes, or literary characters—endless possibilities!

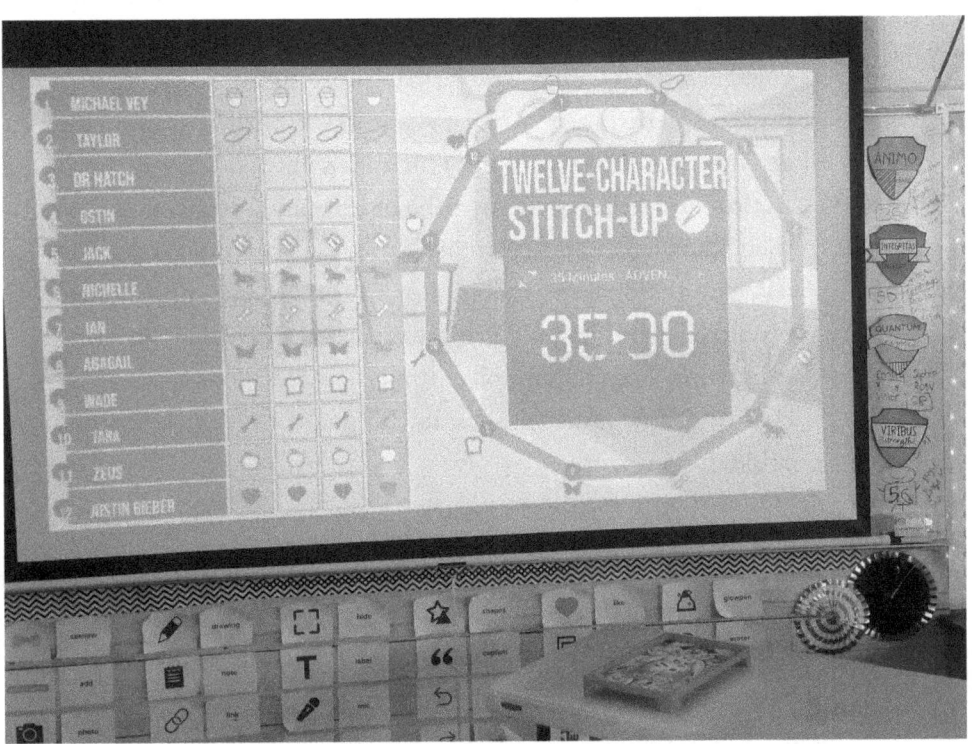

UDL for the Win

Whether you're using the physical Operation game board or not, Twelve-Topic Stitch-Up is guaranteed to leave your class in stitches! This activity engages all learners by blending teamwork, hilarious moments, and hands-on fun with multiple means of engagement, representation, and expression.

- **Engagement** (the *why* of learning): This activity keeps students motivated with its dynamic, high-stakes gameplay. The gamified structure ensures active participation, while the possibility of wild-card concepts and creative themes sparks curiosity and joy.
- **Representation** (the *what* of learning): Through visual mapping, written connections, and team collaboration, students engage with content in varied, meaningful ways. Starter prompts, sentence stems, or visual aids can further scaffold the activity, ensuring accessibility for all learners.
- **Action and expression** (the *how* of learning): Teams showcase their knowledge and creativity as they map connections and navigate the operating table. Rotating roles and collaborative problem-solving highlight individual strengths while fostering teamwork. Sharing completed maps or connections in a celebratory showcase reinforces learning and helps students feel pride in their work.

QUESTIONS FOR DISCUSSION

1. This chapter emphasized that small choices become big choices in both recovery and learning. Reflect on your classroom environment. Where might you offer students small, meaningful opportunities to choose their path (e.g., task formats, difficulty levels, or collaboration partners)? How can these choices gradually build momentum for deeper engagement and growth?
2. The Bjorks' concept of desirable difficulties highlights the importance of challenges that push learners to grow stronger. In your current practice, how do you balance productive struggle with appropriate support? What are some ways you can introduce techniques like spaced repetition, interleaving, or retrieval practice to make struggle both purposeful and rewarding?

3. The Rule of Two encourages teachers to focus on their weakest areas as an opportunity for growth. Reflect on your teaching practice. What are your current growth zones (e.g., technology integration, timely feedback, or innovative teaching strategies)? What specific steps can you take this month to address them while leveraging your existing strengths?

*IT HAPPENS EVERY TIME,
THEY ALL BECOME
BLUEBERRIES.*

— WILLY WONKA

CHAPTER 6

LEAD THE MACHINE

AI, AUTOMATION, AND EDUCATOR JUDGMENT

The Facebook ads made it look like the event of the year.

In February 2024, Willy's Chocolate Experience promised to whisk the people of Glasgow into a world of pure imagination—straight out of a movie.

The ads painted a picture of a hyperrealistic candy paradise: rivers of molten cocoa, lollipop forests, gumdrop lanes, and an entire day immersed in Roald Dahl's whimsical world. Part immersive experience, part all-you-can-eat sugar rush, it sounded like every kid's dream—and, let's face it, most adults' too. Families eagerly shelled out thirty-five pounds a head for their golden tickets.

Excitement was palpable. Children arrived in costume, buzzing with anticipation. This was it.

But instead of a magical wonderland, attendees found themselves in . . . well, a dystopian nightmare, home to nothing but jelly beans and broken dreams.

The "factory" was a barren warehouse in a sketchy part of town. Its decor? A half-inflated balloon arch and a flimsy plastic bridge. The candy forest? A few screen-printed bedsheets as backdrops. The endless sweets? A folding table with half-filled cups of instant lemonade.

And the staff? A handful of well-meaning but wholly untrained day players, given nonsensical scripts just hours before opening. The gibberish dialogue included one particularly baffling character called the Unknown, a silver-masked baddie said to haunt the factory's walls. At random intervals, the Unknown would leap out at terrified children, jack-in-the-box style, delivering cryptic warnings about . . . well, nobody was entirely sure.

But the pièce de résistance—the haunting image that would circulate across the internet like wildfire—was that of a lone actress in a flimsy Oompa-Loompa costume, seated at the refreshment table and staring blankly into the crowd. Her solemn task? To dole out one jelly bean per child to anyone still willing—or desperate enough—to approach her.

Instead of a golden ticket to wonder, attendees found themselves trapped in a chocolate-coated fever dream gone horribly wrong. Kids cried. Parents demanded refunds. Chaos escalated until police were called to shut the whole thing down.

"This is the stuff of nightmares," one horrified parent told reporters as news outlets swarmed the event to document its spectacular implosion.

The mastermind? An AI-generated ad campaign that looked too good to be true—because, of course, it was.

To be fair, the warning signs were there for the eagle-eyed. The promotional materials, while glitzy, were riddled with absurd typos and bizarre nonsense words. The actors, bless their hearts, were just as hapless. Kirsty Paterson, the sad Oompa-Loompa who went viral, later revealed she found the job on Indeed.com. It was offering five hundred pounds for two days of work. She was handed her costume—an Amazon box special—an hour before the event.

And the script? It too was delivered at the eleventh hour. Paul Connell, cast as the off-brand Willy Wonka, described it as "fifteen pages of AI-generated gibberish," including a finale where the masked villain was to be tricked into getting themselves sucked up into an oversized vacuum cleaner (how this was all supposed to happen, of course, was still anybody's guess).

As refunds poured in, the event's organizers—House of Illuminati, led by an enigmatic figure named Billy Coull—vanished into obscurity faster than you could say "Everlasting Gobstopper." But not before leaving a rather incriminating trail of fraudulent gingerbread crumbs behind. Coull, a self-proclaimed entrepreneur and "rising star in the literary world," had apparently self-published seventeen books in the summer of 2023.

And yes, every single one was entirely AI-generated.

Once word of the elaborate con reached the blogosphere and mainstream media, critics had a field day skewering the event as a prime example of everything wrong with AI today. The headlines came rolling in, each one more scathing than the last.

VentureBeat: "Willy Wonka Experience Glasgow: A Metaphor for the Overpromises of AI?"[26]

PR Week: "'Willy Wonka' Experience: A Warning to PRs on AI."[27]

---

26 Carl Franzen, "Willy Wonka Experience Glasgow: A Metaphor for the Overpromises of AI?," VentureBeat, February 24, 2024, https://venturebeat.com/ai/willy-wonka-experience-glasgow-a-metaphor-for-the-overpromises-of-ai/.

27 Aimée Jacobs, "'Willy Wonka' Experience: A Warning to PRs on AI," *PRWeek*, accessed September 25, 2025, https://www.prweek.co.uk/article/1863176/willy-wonka-experience-warning-prs-ai.

Daily Dot: "An 'Immersive' Willy Wonka Kids Experience Left Parents Fuming—Claiming Its Misleading Ads Were the Work of AI." [28]

But here's the thing: This isn't a story about AI's failure—it's a case study in human misuse. The AI didn't plan the event or choose to distribute the nonsense script; people did.

In classrooms, the parallels are striking. Dazzling tech tools or new curriculum ideas may promise the world but fall flat due to poor design or lack of intentionality. No amount of technical wizardry can replace thoughtful design and meaningful engagement. Whether it's a "magical" new tech tool, an AI-enhanced lesson, or a cutting-edge curriculum, the issue isn't artificial intelligence—it's the lack of thoughtful human application.

With hindsight, it's easy to mock the organizers or the parents who fell for the scam. But the real lesson is clear: AI is neither good nor bad on its own. Its value lies entirely in how we use it. What if—just maybe—the fault, dear Brutus, lies not in our AI, but in ourselves?

Think you could do better at spotting AI in action? Let's put that confidence to the test.

Take a look at the image displayed here: fifteen faces, a diverse array of individuals spanning different ages, races, and backgrounds. But not everything is as it seems.

Study each face carefully, for there may or may not be a few AI-generated portraits lurking in the mix. Your job is to figure out who's real and who's not.

What should you look for? Be on guard for telltale signs of forgery—a smile that's just a little too perfect, glasses that don't sit quite right, an extra appendage, backgrounds that feel warped or inconsistent.

You've got two minutes. Work solo or team up with a sharp-eyed friend to decide: Which of these faces—if any—are the work of AI?

Ready? Grab your pencil, set the timer, and have at it!

---

28 Marlon Ettinger, "An 'Immersive' Willy Wonka Kids Experience Left Parents Fuming—Claiming Its Misleading Ads Were the Work of AI," Daily Dot, August 4, 2025, https://www.dailydot.com/news/willy-wonka-experience-ai/.

Okay, gang, time's up. Let's see how we did.

If you said that the woman in photo A was an AI fraud, give yourself a pat on the back! Those shady sunglasses are a dead giveaway. And if you spotted the faraway look in the eye of the dapper gentleman in photo E? Good on you—that one's a fake too.

In fact, they all are.

Believe it or not, there's not a single real person among the lineup that you just reviewed: Every single one of the fifteen faces was entirely generated by AI using a free website called ThisPersonDoesNotExist.com.

Shocked?

Don't be. If you struggled to determine whether a person's image was real or AI-generated, you're in very good company. A recent study conducted by researchers at the University of Waterloo revealed that people found it surprisingly challenging to distinguish between the faces of real individuals and those that were created by artificial intelligence. In fact, the study revealed that more than 40 percent of the time, folks consistently believe that non-AI faces were, in fact, generated by artificial intelligence, while the fakes have gotten so convincing that we're actually more inclined to believe they're the real McCoy.[29]

Now think about this in the context of your classroom. The same challenge of spotting AI is already happening with student writing. With tools like ChatGPT, student submissions are often polished enough to raise suspicion, but the truth can be nearly impossible to verify. Complicating matters further, AI-powered AI detectors or originality reports are almost universally unreliable. And if that's not enough, free tools like Undetectable AI's Humanizer function can remove all detectable traces of AI usage from a piece of writing nearly instantly—essentially a digital game of cat and click-of-the-mouse.

The implications for educators are profound. How do we evaluate authenticity in an age when AI can mimic human output so convincingly? How do we balance the opportunities AI provides with the responsibility to teach students about ethical and transparent use of technology?

This isn't just a game; it's the reality of education in the digital age. The lesson isn't about fearing AI but understanding how to use it thoughtfully while equipping students to do the same.

But before we dive deeper, let's consider the broader picture. How do we ensure that AI serves as a tool for learning and engagement, not just a shortcut? To answer this, we turn to a trusted framework for evaluating technology in education. And to find it, it looks like we're headed back to Harvard.

---

29 Andreea Pocol, et al., "Seeing Is No Longer Believing: A Survey on the State of Deepfakes, AI-Generated Humans, and Other Nonveridical Media," in *Advances in Computer Graphics: 40th Computer Graphics International Conference, CGI 2023, Shanghai, China, August 28–September 1, 2023, Proceedings, Part II*, eds. Bin Sheng, Lei Bi, and Jinman Kim (Springer-Verlag, 2023), 427–440, https://www.researchgate.net/publication/376952258_Seeing_is _No_Longer_Believing_A_Survey_on_the_State_of_Deepfakes_AI-Generated_Humans _and_Other_Nonveridical_Media.

THE GAME'S AFOOT

In 2010, Dr. Ruben Puentedura, then a former Harvard teaching fellow and now a world-renowned expert in technology and education, developed the SAMR model to help educators evaluate and enhance their use of technology. His work emphasizes the belief that not all tech integration—or indeed all tech—is created equal. Simply adding a digital tool or an AI enhancement to a lesson doesn't automatically improve outcomes. Instead, Puentedura invites educators to view technology as a vessel for deeper, more transformative learning experiences, helping us venture further into uncharted waters at every stage of the SAMR framework.

The SAMR model breaks down into four stages: substitution, augmentation, modification, and redefinition. At the substitution level, technology acts as a direct replacement—like swapping a paper map for GPS or climbing into a rowboat to gaze down into shallow waters just off the shore. It's helpful, but the core task remains unchanged. Augmentation takes us further, like popping on a pair of goggles and a snorkel to see beneath the surface more clearly and comfortably. But

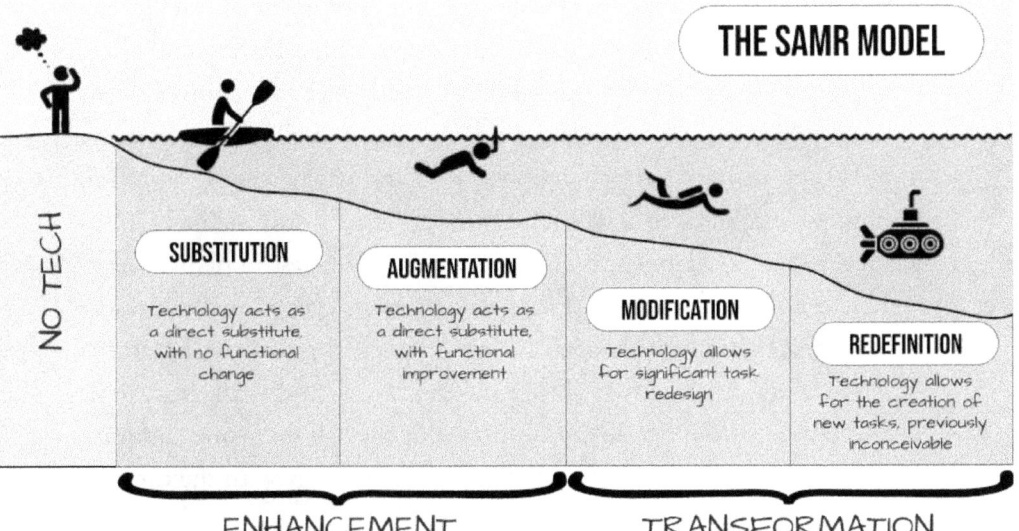

starting at the modification stage, technology has the power to transform the task itself, akin to strapping on scuba gear to explore a vibrant coral reef up close. Finally, at the redefinition level, technology enables experiences previously unimaginable, like piloting a deep-sea submarine to uncover the mysteries of the ocean floor. SAMR isn't just about using as much tech as we can—it's about discovering how far the tech can take us.

For classroom teachers, the challenge lies in evaluating AI tools and determining which level of the SAMR model best aligns with a lesson's goals while addressing the unique needs of students. Many edtech tools promise faster grading or feedback, but replacing yesterday's Scantrons with today's AI-assisted quizzes doesn't prepare students for the future. (Once again, Kahoot! comes to mind. Sorry—that's our last jab in their direction, we promise.) As we've seen time and again, this fully automated approach risks prioritizing convenience over critical thinking. And as the Willy Wonka fiasco and the AI face experiment make clear, the devil is always in the details. Meaningful learning requires more than just surface-level solutions.

So instead of prizing AI for its breakneck speed and automated efficiency, let's take a closer look at a series of instructional approaches that seamlessly blend the incredible capabilities of artificial intelligence with the irreplaceable elements of human teaching. Throughout these examples, we'll use Dr. Puentedura's SAMR model as a common lens through which we can explore the possibilities that all sorts of exciting new AI tools can offer our classrooms, we'll and pay particular attention to how we can keep ourselves (and our students) firmly at the helm of whatever ships we happen to be sailing in our daily lesson plans.

Here are three AI-infused case studies from exceptional educators who turned thoughtful theory into action-packed practice. They teach different grade levels, cover diverse content areas, and work in schools in different locations across the country. But they all share one common thread: a masterful balance of cutting-edge technology with the timeless principles of student-centered instruction. Great teaching, as we'll see, always transcends subject and setting.

WHICH OF THE IMAGES SHOWN HERE WOULD MAKE THE BEST CHOICE? EXPLAIN YOUR THINKING.

A HIGH SCHOOL ENGLISH CLASS GETS ANIMATED

In this first case study, Nicole Schuyler, a high school English teacher from Arlington, Virginia, elevated a standard unit on Ernest Hemingway by using the AI image creation tool DALL-E to produce a series of thought-provoking visuals. Her deceptively simple question to students was this: If Hemingway were choosing one of these eight images for the cover of his short story collection, which would he pick and why?

At first glance, this activity seems straightforward, but it exemplifies a powerful approach to student learning—prioritizing the process of close reading, analysis, and critical thinking over a tidy, singular answer. By encouraging her students to explain their reasoning, the teacher creates space for rich interpretations and classroom discussions, all rooted in the same principles of close textual analysis they'd been practicing with Hemingway's fiction.

Students noticed details that were both obvious and deeply symbolic. Some pointed out that many of the soldiers in the images were clearly plastic toys, which seemed to echo their smallness and disposability within the larger machinery of war—a theme that runs throughout Hemingway's writing on the dehumanizing impact of combat.

Others homed in on the fact that a few soldiers had their backs turned to the viewer. To these students, it felt like a visual metaphor for the way soldiers felt abandoned by their countries or societies. This was a painful parallel to the postwar disillusionment of the Lost Generation, which Hemingway likewise captures so vividly in his work.

Still others zeroed in on details like mangled faces or distorted features, offering that these stylistic choices mirrored how war erased the individual identity of its participants—another recurring theme in the stories they'd studied.

The brilliance of this activity lies in how it leverages AI to create opportunities for deep thinking with minimal time investment from the teacher. Instead of spending hours scouring photo archives for school-appropriate images, the teacher generated a variety of compelling, conversation-sparking visuals in seconds. This low-impact, high-yield use of AI fits squarely into the augmentation level of the SAMR model: It enhances the learning experience without altering the core objective of developing critical analysis skills.

Where SAMR begins to push toward modification, however, is in how AI transforms the task itself. By engaging students in a deeper visual analysis that links close reading with creative interpretation, the assignment challenges them to grapple with Hemingway's themes in ways that suddenly feel both wholly authentic and personally resonant. It's no longer just about what Hemingway wrote—it's about how his words translate visually and interact with modern interpretations.

This exercise also models the importance of thoughtful, open-ended questioning. Instead of simply asking for plot summaries or predefined answers, Mrs. Schuyler encouraged her students to wrestle with ambiguity, draw connections, and articulate their interpretations. The images themselves were not the final product; the students' thinking and discussion were. By prioritizing the process over the product, this activity celebrated the iterative nature of learning, avoiding the trap of pigeonholing learners into a single correct response and instead deepening everyone's understanding by inviting diverse perspectives.

Say . . . that sounds an awful lot like UDL!

In short, this lesson is a shining example of how teachers can use AI to enrich the universal accessibility of their instruction, enhance student engagement, and push critical thinking to new depths. With the click of a mouse, technology provided an accessible starting point for student-driven inquiry—reminding us how UDL and SAMR together help us navigate uncharted waters where deeper understanding awaits.

(And we're just getting started!)

ZOMBIES INVADE A SEVENTH-GRADE MATH CLASS

In this second case study, Jad Taylor, a middle school math teacher from Buffalo, New York, used AI to breathe life into an otherwise ordinary lesson on ratios—with a little brainy help from the undead. Inspired by his students' love of pop culture—Taylor Swift concerts and zombies—Mr.

Taylor began by asking an AI writing tool to help him generate a basic word problem about ratios. The result? "A recipe calls for two cups of flour to make twelve cookies. If you want to make twenty-four cookies, how many cups of flour will you need?"

The math worked, but let's be honest—the word problem still had all the excitement of a soggy cardboard box. So the teacher pushed the AI to think bigger. He reframed the problem as something his students couldn't resist: a zombie outbreak at a sold-out Taylor Swift concert. That request produced this: "Suppose that a zombie outbreak starts with one infected individual at a Taylor Swift concert in a crowded football stadium with a capacity of eighty thousand people. If the rate of infection spreads at five people per minute and the concert lasts two hours, how many people will be infected by the end?"

Better, but Mr. Taylor wasn't finished. He went back to the AI with one final request—lean into the theming this time, and really make it spooky, silly, and attention-grabbing. The AI delivered: "THEY'RE AFTER YOUR BRAAAAAINS! Oh no, a horde of zombies just crashed Taylor Swift's concert at a packed football stadium! The stadium holds eighty thousand screaming fans, and the zombies are spreading fast, infecting five new people every minute. Can you figure out how many unlucky concertgoers will become zombies by the end of the concert? The concert lasts two hours, so you'd better solve this problem fast before it's too late . . . MWAHAHAHA!"

Bingo.

With the problem perfectly themed, Mr. Taylor turned to an AI image generation tool to create a dramatic, stadium-style zombie scene—no more digging through endless stock photos. A few clicks, a quick copy and paste, and he had a slide that looked like it belonged on a movie poster. This would be exactly the sort of word problem that a clever group of seventh graders couldn't wait to solve.

The result wasn't just a better problem; it was a hook that connected directly to his students' pop culture interests while supporting mathematical learning goals like applying proportional reasoning and scaling.

And by leaning into student interests and offering multiple pathways for problem-solving, Mr. Taylor's approach aligned with UDL's emphasis on engagement and representation—making math feel relevant, accessible, and fun for all learners.

But the real magic came next. Mr. Taylor didn't stop with one themed word problem; he transformed the entire lesson into a can't-miss event. To set the stage, he queued up the theme song from *The Walking Dead* on YouTube, and for good measure, he came to class dressed in his best Rick Grimes costume, immediately captivating his learners (take that, Willy Wonka!). Students' imaginations immediately ran wild.

After solving the sample zombie outbreak conundrum, they broke into teams, brainstorming all kinds of similarly inspired word problems with over-the-top scenarios of their own: pirate battles, haunted houses, superhero rescues. Whatever their imaginations conjured up, Mr. Taylor guided his students' ideas, using the AI tools where appropriate to help flesh out the corresponding visuals of the word problems. One team created a haunted house problem, exploring proportional measurements for eerie room layouts, while another team tackled superhero rescues that involved calculating the time and distance required to blast across Metropolis (using the very real landmarks, locations, and geographic coordinates of New York City as their starting point!). In real time, students saw their imaginations brought to life through quick, polished prompts they were excited to share with their classmates.

This is where the zombified math lesson landed firmly at the modification level of the SAMR model. Technology didn't just enhance the activity; it transformed it. AI tools allowed Mr. Taylor to reimagine a mundane concept like ratios into an engaging, student-centered experience that connected directly to his learners' interests. More importantly, it modeled the creative, iterative process of refining ideas—a skill that students carried over into their own work.

Here, the focus shifted away from simply solving word problems to creating them. Students worked collaboratively to craft, iterate, and test their ideas while demonstrating curiosity, critical thinking, and math mastery. And while the AI certainly came along for the ride, it never once put the teaching or learning on autopilot.

By not taking himself too seriously, Mr. Taylor inspired his students to take their learning more seriously than ever before. This is where AI and human ingenuity intersect, where technology helps us go deeper instead of faster, and where learning feels every bit as exciting as an iconic pop star concert and a zombie apocalypse (without any of the real-life danger).

FIFTH-GRADE STUDENTS BOLDLY GO WHERE NO CLASS HAS GONE BEFORE

Kaitlynn Greenstein's Mission to Mars project is a perfect example of the SAMR model in action, showing how technology not only enhances the learning experience but completely redefines what's possible in the classroom. In her fifth-grade STEM class at Woodside Elementary in Glen Burnie, Maryland, Mrs. Greenstein kicked off her unit by introducing her students to "7 Minutes of Terror"—a gripping NASA video

that chronicles the tense moments of a Mars rover's entry, descent, and landing. The hook was simple but powerful: What does it take to engineer a successful rover landing?

From this spark, a dynamic thirteen-week STEM challenge took shape. The centerpiece? A coded navigation challenge featuring Dash robots as student-built "rovers" navigating a simulated Martian maze made of masking tape. This wasn't just a static activity; every part of the lesson subtly incorporated gamified elements and clever touches of AI to increase engagement while pushing students into deeper waters of critical thinking and problem-solving.

Teams worked collaboratively to program their rovers, refining their code over weeks of beta testing and iteration. The maze itself offered meaningful choice with multiple pathways: Safer routes were straightforward but slow, while riskier narrow passageways offered faster times but higher stakes. Students strategized, experimented, and ultimately learned to weigh risks and rewards—a hallmark of the modification stage in SAMR, where technology redesigns the task to challenge learners in new ways.

On launch day, the fifth-grade classroom transformed into mission control. Nervous excitement filled the air as teams lined up to execute their rover runs. Every second mattered: Precision coding and collaborative planning were the only paths to success. A massive scoreboard tracked team results, adding a subtle competitive edge, and penalties for crossing maze boundaries created real-time consequences for missteps. And when a rover successfully navigated the maze, the entire class erupted into applause—celebrating effort, teamwork, and learning.

What made this unit so powerful wasn't just the technology. It was the process. Students weren't just coding for coding's sake; they were living the role of engineers, refining their work at every step, and reflecting on both successes and failures. After the culminating runs, Mrs. Greenstein facilitated a class debrief where students shared coding strategies, identified challenges, and brainstormed improvements. It was a lesson in perseverance and problem-solving, grounded in real-world application.

And then came the greatest human element of them all: Mrs. Greenstein's father, a real NASA engineer, joined the class to share his experiences, answer questions, and inspire students to see themselves in future STEM careers. This personal connection, paired with the high-tech tools of robotics and coding, transformed the unit into something that transcended the walls of the classroom—a once-in-a-lifetime experience that redefined what these fifth graders believed they could achieve.

In terms of the SAMR model, this Mission to Mars journey represents every bit of the redefinition stage, where technology enables experiences that were previously unimaginable. Coding Dash robots, navigating a gamified maze, and giving students an inroad to the very same people and skills that make real-world engineering challenges come to life? This connected the kids to the content more deeply than an AI-generated video or automated multiple-choice test ever could.

The brilliance of this example lies in its emphasis on the process rather than the final product. Students tackled desired difficulties, reflected on setbacks, and celebrated their learning—just as NASA engineers would. By leveraging technology to create a rich, dynamic experience, Mrs. Greenstein provided her students with a launchpad not just to explore STEM concepts but to develop curiosity, creativity, and resilience. Moreover, this project exemplifies the very best of UDL by integrating real-world applications, scaffolding teamwork, and offering diverse roles—from coding to strategizing—ensuring every student found a meaningful way to contribute.

This is where technology and human-centered teaching converge, creating deeper, more meaningful learning experiences that are out of this world (sorry, we couldn't resist!).

A PLAYBOOK FOR SAMR SUCCESS

This chapter's playbook highlights dynamic activities that seamlessly blend cutting-edge AI tools with timeless teaching practices, gamified engagement, and playful pedagogy. These examples go beyond simply replacing tasks with technology—they amplify meaning, deepen rigor, and transform what's possible in the classroom by creating the kinds of lessons that students won't want to cheat on or miss.

As always, the focus is on technique before technology. Each activity showcases how thoughtful design can bring the stages of the SAMR model to life, moving beyond mere substitution to create rich, student-centered experiences where AI doesn't just enhance learning—it supercharges engagement.

But great teaching isn't just about integrating technology. It's about making it work for every learner, in ways that feel like play. That's where UDL and playful pedagogy collide. SAMR challenges us to push past surface-level tech use and into deeper waters. UDL ensures that every student—regardless of background, learning style, or cognitive ability—can meaningfully engage in that learning. And playful pedagogy? That's the secret sauce. It's the element that turns good lessons into irresistible, game-inspired experiences.

Every activity in this chapter is designed to leverage AI through SAMR, provide multiple pathways for learning through UDL, and infuse play to make lessons as fun as they are effective. The best technology isn't just powerful; it's purposeful, playful, and primed for engagement.

HAPPY GREEN BOXES

Game On

Writing can feel intimidating, but Happy Green Boxes turns the process into a dynamic, engaging experience that celebrates growth every step of the way, Wordle style! In this activity, students work collaboratively in a shared Google Slides presentation, starting with neutral gray boxes representing each facet of their written submissions (these could be one box per sentence, one box per paragraph, or one box per question based on the needs of your lesson). As the activity progresses, teachers gradually provide real-time feedback simply by color-coding each box—changing from gray to yellow to green.

This activity fosters desired difficulty, immediate tech-powered feedback loops, and meaningful teacher interactions that help students feel seen, heard, and validated in their writing journey.

A SAMR-Ready Upgrade

This enhances traditional writing prompts by helping teachers and students forge meaningful connections through using tech tools!

Quick-Start Guide

1. **Set the scene:** Begin with a shared Google Slides template containing one slide (or row) per student and a series of gray boxes for their responses. Each student claims a row or slide and types their answers to a teacher-provided prompt directly into their designated boxes.
2. **Give live feedback:** As students write, teachers evaluate submissions in real time. Feedback is given both verbally and visually simply by changing the box colors.
    - **Gray:** Initial submission
    - **Yellow:** Almost there—needs guidance to refine ideas
    - **Green:** Nailed it—a polished, thoughtful response
3. **Collaborate and revise:** Encourage peer feedback or collaborative edits, prompting students to refer to work that's been singled out as particularly high quality. This will help all students see plenty of real-time examples and push their thinking to refine their submissions as they aim for those coveted green boxes.

Pedagogy Power-Up

Happy Green Boxes exemplifies SAMR by transforming traditional writing feedback into a real-time, collaborative process. Replacing handwritten notes with digital slides is substitution. Enhancing clarity through color-coded progress indicators is augmentation. Allowing for peer learning and collective revisions is modification. And the iterative feedback loop transforms writing into an interactive experience that celebrates progress and mastery, fostering a vibrant classroom culture where effort and growth are front and center. That's redefinition!

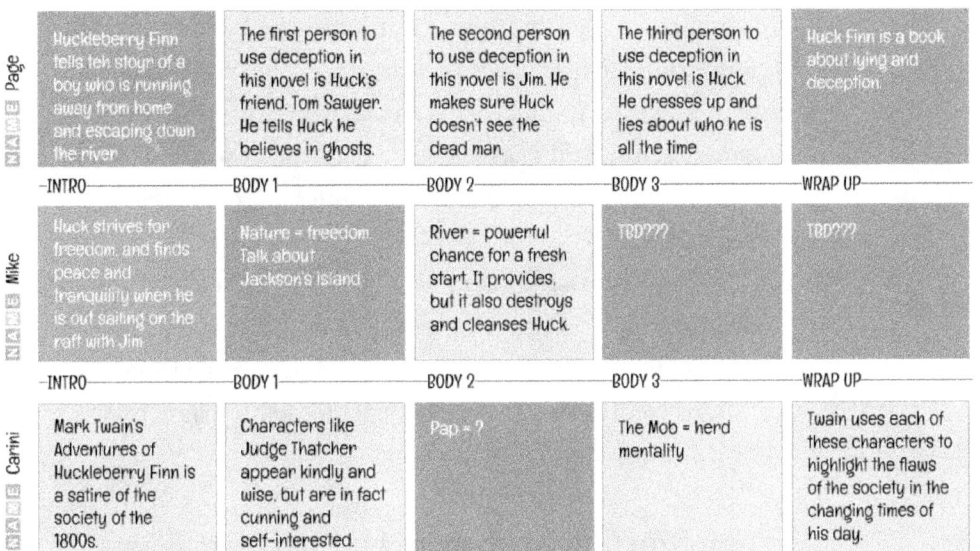

House Rules

- **Make it competitive:** Split the class into teams (with a certain number of slides per team) and track how many green boxes each team earns by the end of the session.
- **Add a theme:** Turn the boxes into a themed progression (e.g., from rocks to gems for geology or from seedling to bloom for a biology lesson).
- **Leverage AI:** Use tools like ChatGPT to generate writing prompts or to provide sample responses for students to critique.

UDL for the Win

Happy Green Boxes is more than just a writing activity—it's a celebration of the iterative process of learning. With clear, constructive feedback at every step, students gain confidence, refine their skills, and deepen their understanding in a supportive, playful environment.

- **Engagement** (the *why* of learning): Real-time feedback energizes students, creating a sense of accomplishment and investment in their progress. The gamified structure keeps motivation high and ensures every student feels supported and celebrated.
- **Representation** (the *what* of learning): The visual feedback system provides immediate, accessible insights into student progress, helping all learners see where they excel and where they can improve. Peer-reviewed examples offer concrete models for improvement.
- **Action and expression** (the *how* of learning): Flexible formats (individual, peer editing, or group work) allow students to engage in ways that suit their needs. Iterative revisions and scaffolded feedback empower students to demonstrate mastery while building confidence in their skills.

POKÉVOLVE TRADING CARD CREATOR

Game On

Who says studying has to be boring? In the Pokévolve Trading Card Creator activity, students transform course content into colorful, collectible trading cards inspired by Pokémon-style evolution. Whether it's a historical figure, a scientific concept, or a literary character, students illustrate growth and change over three distinct stages of evolution—each one showcasing their learning in creative, engaging ways.

This activity taps into multiple pathways for expression: Students can draw their creatures, browse free AI art libraries, or use AI image generation tools with teacher support to bring their ideas to life. The result? An unforgettable learning experience that blends creativity, content knowledge, and technology into one dynamic package.

A SAMR-Ready Upgrade

This improves the usual student-created study guide by focusing on how a single character, place, or concept can evolve over time.

Quick-Start Guide

1. **Set the scene:** Start by introducing students to the activity. They will be designing a series of Pokémon-style trading cards that reflect the evolution of a single character, concept, or idea studied in class. Examples could include Abraham Lincoln evolving from Baybraham to Warprez, a literary figure like Jay Gatsby transforming across key moments in the novel, or a scientific process like photosynthesis unfolding in stages.
2. **Provide templates:** You can find free online templates for creating these cards (or similar templates for other popular trading card games like Magic: The Gathering) with a simple Google search. Then break it down. Each card the students create will include:
    c. Stage name: A fun, creative title for each stage of evolution
    d. Abilities: Special powers or traits linked to the character/concept
    e. Weaknesses: Challenges or limitations the character/concept faces
    f. Artwork: Hand-drawn illustrations, AI-generated images, or online artwork that visually represents each stage
7. **Evolve the content:** Here's where students get creative with their knowledge.
    h. Stage 1 (basic form): This is the starting point. Introduce the core traits of the character or concept.
    i. Stage 2 (intermediate): Highlight growth, conflict, or transformation.
    j. Stage 3 (final evolution): Showcase the peak evolution—where the concept reaches its full potential.

Pedagogy Power-Up

This activity isn't just fun—it's powerful. At its core, the Pokévolve Trading Card Creator aligns beautifully with the SAMR model by turning basic note-taking into a multidimensional creative process. Substitution is achieved through trading cards replacing static study guides, while the visual and written elements deepen understanding through augmentation. As students chart the evolution of their subjects, they use higher-order thinking, hitting the modification level. Redefinition comes alive when AI tools enable unique artistic interpretations, allowing students to merge creativity with deep content knowledge in ways previously unimaginable.

House Rules

- **Collaborate in teams:** Divide students into groups to create multicard sets. This encourages teamwork and shared creativity.
- **Add a competitive twist:** Host a gallery walk where students vote on the most creative designs, best abilities, or strongest connections to course content.
- **Theme it up:** Tie the activity to class content—evolve literary heroes, scientific processes, or historical events.

- **Leverage AI:** Use AI image generators to add a modern twist, but give students the option to draw or source free artwork too. Teachers can drive the AI tools based on student input to ensure focus and learning remain front and center.

UDL for the Win

The Pokévolve Trading Card Creator is one of our favorite ways to "catch 'em all" by combining visual, written, and hands-on elements to foster all kinds of engagement. It encourages students to represent ideas in accessible ways, it promotes collaboration, and it allows them to demonstrate mastery in formats that celebrate creativity and individuality.

- **Engagement** (the *why* of learning): The creative, gamified structure keeps students energized and curious. By choosing characters or concepts they find compelling, students connect personally with the material, boosting investment and enjoyment.
- **Representation** (the *what* of learning): Diverse options for visual, verbal, and written expression cater to all learners. Scaffolded templates and teacher-provided examples ensure accessibility for students at different skill levels.
- **Action and expression** (the *how* of learning): Flexible formats for content creation—drawing, AI art, or presourced visuals—allow students to showcase knowledge in ways that resonate with their strengths and interests, reinforcing mastery through iterative design.

HEXAGON HUNTERS

Game On

What if a page of printed material could become a massive, immersive game board? Hexagon Hunters makes it possible, empowering teachers to create custom oversized game boards using AI-powered image rasterization. By overlaying a hexagon grid onto any image, teachers can design engaging, interactive review activities that blend learning with gameplay.

Here's how it works: Students work independently in teams to solve course-related questions, and every set of five correct answers earns them a chance to move their team's player token across the hexagon board. Bonus spaces and wild cards scattered throughout the board keep the gameplay fresh and strategic, while the constant flow of problem-solving keeps every team engaged.

This isn't just a review—it's an epic classroom quest where every answer gets a student closer to victory.

A SAMR-Ready Upgrade

This transforms traditional review activities into dynamic, team-based board games with the help of a free AI tool.

Quick-Start Guide

1. **Set the scene:** Choose an image relevant to your lesson. It could be a historical map, a scientific diagram, or something whimsical like a fantasy castle. Insert the image into Google Slides and overlay a grid of hexagons, shaped much like a honeycomb. Designate specific hexagons as bonus spaces that give students things like extra points, power-ups, or wild cards.
2. **Create a board:** Once you're happy with how your game board looks, hop on over to your favorite search engine and look for a free image rasterizer. The magic of this AI-powered tool is that it will instantly allow you to upscale your standard-sized printout into a massive multipage poster that's crystal clear!
3. **Explain the rules:** Students work in teams to solve problems, complete questions, or meet other teacher-set tasks (e.g., defining vocabulary or solving math problems). After completing five tasks, they call over the teacher to verify their answers. Upon your

approval, they roll a die to determine how far they can move on the hexagon grid.

4. **Keep the action moving:** Teams race to collect points by landing on designated spaces. Here's how they break down:

   e. Point hexagons: Earn points for your team simply by passing through these spaces at any time during your turn.

   f. Wild-card hexagons: Land on one of these spaces to collect a card that offers strategic advantages, like stealing points from rivals or protecting against attacks.

   g. Dice hexagons: Finish your turn here to gain an extra dice roll.

   h. Safe-zone hexagons: Parking your token here gives your team the chance to bank points strategically, preventing them from being stolen or lost due to any subsequent interference from rival teams.

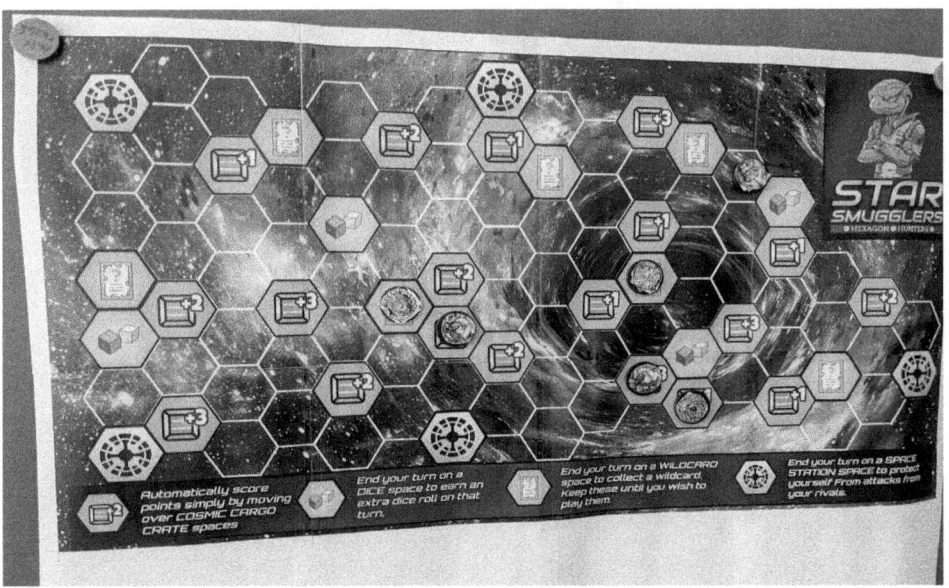

Keep in mind that since every team is working asynchronously to solve the assigned problems, there is never any time wasted waiting for their turn! Encourage collaboration and problem-solving as students revisit questions to keep earning turns again and again in an endless state of flow.

Pedagogy Power-Up

Hexagon Hunters leverages SAMR to transform rote review into a high-energy collaborative quest. At the substitution level, you're replacing traditional worksheets with digital board games. With minimal prep, the activity is augmenting traditional note-taking with strategic gameplay and visual elements to enhance engagement. Tasks that were once completed individually now enjoy a new level of modification as students take part in problem-solving as a collaborative team effort. And the rasterized images you've created with free AI tools immediately redefine review days by welcoming your learners into a world that is immersive and full of tailored, content-rich adventures.

House Rules

- **Make it competitive:** Track team progress on a leaderboard and reward creative gameplay.
- **Add themes:** Tailor the activity to your unit. You could create a galactic smuggling adventure for physics or a treasure hunt for world history.
- **Leverage AI:** Use AI tools to create custom backgrounds or overlays that match your game's theme—then laminate your game board (or slide individual printed pages into plastic page protectors) and save it for when you want to play again!

UDL for the Win

By anchoring all three UDL pillars into its design, Hexagon Hunters delivers a collaborative, content-rich experience that keeps students engaged and learning dynamically. Ready to hunt for those hexagons? Let the game begin!

- **Engagement** (the *why* of learning): The gamified structure, combined with thematic elements, energizes students and fosters teamwork. Competition against the clock and between teams keeps engagement high, while collaborative problem-solving ensures no one is left behind.
- **Representation** (the *what* of learning): The activity combines verbal, visual, and hands-on modalities, making content accessible to all learners. Scaffolding through team roles and teacher guidance supports diverse needs.
- **Action and expression** (the *how* of learning): The flexibility of gameplay ensures students can contribute in ways that suit their strengths, from strategizing to solving problems or rolling dice. Success is celebrated as a team, reinforcing collaboration and collective achievement.

QUESTIONS FOR DISCUSSION

1. The Willy's Chocolate Experience fiasco underscores the risks of relying on AI without intentionality. How can you balance efficiency with thoughtfulness in your use of technology, ensuring it enhances learning rather than detracts from it?
2. The SAMR model highlights the potential of technology to transform learning experiences. Reflect on a current or past lesson. How might you elevate it to the modification or redefinition level using AI tools?
3. Of the three teacher case studies featured in this chapter—the thought-provoking Hemingway high school lesson, the seventh graders' AI-powered zombie battle, and the fifth graders' epic Mission to Mars event—which feels most applicable to your teaching practice? How might you adapt these strategies to fit your subject area and classroom?

YOU SHOULDN'T CALL YOURSELF THE MISFIT BECAUSE I KNOW YOU'RE A GOOD MAN AT HEART. I CAN JUST LOOK AT YOU AND TELL.

— FLANNERY O'CONNOR

CHAPTER 7

CULTIVATE THE GOOD

EQUITY, EMPATHY, AND ETHICS

"The grandmother didn't want to go to Florida."
So begins "A Good Man Is Hard to Find," one of the most iconic works of American fiction and the defining short story by Flannery O'Connor, a master of the Southern Gothic genre.

The story follows a dysfunctional family road trip gone disastrously wrong, led by a manipulative, self-righteous matriarch known only as the grandmother. She spends much of the journey reminiscing about the past, lamenting how much simpler and better the world used to be, all while pointing to every sign of its supposed decline. As the family winds through sleepy backroads, O'Connor masterfully builds toward a chilling climax where a chance encounter with an escaped convict forces the grandmother into a moment of reckoning—not just with her fate but with the truths she can no longer outrun. It's an explosive moment where past and future collide.

At its core, the story is a meditation on morality. Not the performative kind that looks good in a church pew or classroom syllabus but the messy, unspoken kind that emerges in crisis. when the stakes are real and the consequences can't be undone. Are good men truly hard to find? Or are we just too eager to label others before truly seeing them for who (or what) they are?

That's the heart of this chapter: how we teach students (and remind ourselves) to hone a moral compass. This is not just to recognize goodness in others but to navigate difficult terrain when the old maps no longer guide us.

In a world of accelerating change, classrooms have become a proving ground for values in action. Whether we're debating new technologies, confronting social injustice, or simply mediating everyday conflicts, educators are no longer just delivering knowledge; we're modeling judgment, fostering empathy, and leading with integrity. And the best way to build those skills isn't through navel-gazing philosophy. It's through practice.

So let's take a little road trip of our own. Let's ask what it means to be "good" in a world that keeps changing. And let's explore how playful, purpose-driven classrooms can help students not just find the right answers but become the kind of "good" people who lead with empathy, integrity, and courage no matter what obstacles they encounter along the way.

In fact, let's go to Florida.

FLORIDA MAN SEES THE FUTURE

At the 2025 Future of Education Technology Conference in Orlando, noted tech visionary Guy Kawasaki took the stage to deliver a keynote address fittingly titled "How to Help People Be Remarkable."

Kawasaki, known for his work as Apple's chief evangelist during the company's meteoric rise—he reported directly to Steve Jobs—has spent decades helping people harness the transformative power of technology. Today, he continues that mission as chief evangelist for Canva, host of the *Remarkable People* podcast, and author of *Think Remarkable*, a book distilling lessons from his own career and hundreds of interviews with extraordinary minds, including Jane Goodall, Neil deGrasse Tyson, and Steve Wozniak.

Kawasaki's message was one of optimism and empowerment, particularly regarding AI's potential in education. But what truly captivated the audience was an unexpected revelation where artificial technology and undeniably human presence combined—leaving thousands of educators in stunned silence.

He began by describing KawasakiGPT, his personal AI assistant. He trained it on everything he's ever written—books, articles, interviews—creating an AI model capable of channeling his voice, ideas, and decades of experience. "It's an even better Guy Kawasaki than Guy Kawasaki," he joked, admitting that he had even consulted KawasakiGPT while preparing the very keynote he was delivering. "I use AI every stinking day. It's not cheating—it's research. It's optimization. It's about being a better version of myself."

Then, with a grin, he dropped a bombshell.

AI or no AI, it was still a flesh-and-blood Guy Kawasaki standing on that stage delivering his first keynote since receiving a cochlear implant. To the total surprise of the audience, he revealed he was legally deaf.

Mic drop.

His revelation wasn't just personal—it was proof. A living demonstration of technology's power to amplify human potential and eliminate barriers through universal design.

"Ideas are easy. Implementation is hard," he reminded the crowd. No matter how powerful technology becomes, it is only as valuable as the ways we choose to use it. The real focus should remain on ideas, innovation, and impact.

But Kawasaki was just as clear-eyed about AI's responsibilities. He challenged educators to foster a "growth mindset and a growth environment"—one where students see AI not as a replacement for effort but as a tool to amplify their abilities, fuel creativity, and strengthen resilience.

And then, pulling no punches, Kawasaki delivered one final knockout. "In the near future, there will be two types of people: losers and those who know how to use AI."

It was a bold, even jarring claim, but his message was clear. AI itself won't take your job, but those who know how to use it effectively will. For leaders and learners alike, the time to act is now. Learn to leverage AI's potential or risk being left behind.

Kawasaki's insights highlight a growing tension in education: How do we balance the need for innovation with the core values of learning?

Nowhere is this more evident than in the starkly opposing stances taken by two of the world's leading academic programs—Advanced Placement (AP) and International Baccalaureate (IB)—on AI's role in the classroom.

As AI makes its mark on K–12 education, these two titans are charting radically different paths. The College Board (AP) bans AI outright, insisting that students must generate all written work independently to uphold traditional assessment values and academic integrity.

IB, in contrast, embraces AI as a learning tool, emphasizing ethical usage and proper attribution rather than prohibition.

This difference raises fundamental questions: Should AI be restricted to preserve traditional academic rigor, or should students be encouraged to use it responsibly as an essential tool for the future?

To be clear, both organizations acknowledge AI is here to stay—but their diverging policies reflect a deeper philosophical divide. AP's approach prioritizes authenticity in student work, seeing AI as a potential threat to academic integrity. IB, meanwhile, views AI as a fundamental shift in knowledge creation, one that necessitates new ways of assessing student learning.

For educators, this debate poses a pressing challenge: Can we integrate AI meaningfully without compromising the core values of education? Or is restricting it the only way to preserve the foundations of academic rigor?

This is where playful pedagogy and UDL deliver a powerful one-two punch. Instead of framing AI as either a threat to traditional learning or a shortcut for students, embracing purposeful play encourages us to explore how AI can expand access, enhance engagement, and provide multiple means of demonstrating understanding.

When implemented thoughtfully, AI can level the playing field, reduce barriers, and create new opportunities for deeper learning—but only if we approach it with intentionality.

As we stand at this crossroads, the choice isn't just about technology; it's about what kind of learning environments (and what kinds of learners) we want to cultivate.

FIVE QUESTIONS FOR A BRIGHTER FUTURE

AI is reshaping the way we teach, learn, and interact in classrooms across the globe. But, as Spider-Man's ever quotable Uncle Ben so wisely reminded us, with great power comes great responsibility.

As educators, we must pause to ask not just how these changes can enhance education but how they align—or conflict—with the timeless values of creating classrooms that can best meet the unique and ever-changing needs of every student we serve.

At the start of this chapter, we saw how Flannery O'Connor's "A Good Man Is Hard to Find" challenged readers to lean into discomfort, asking them to sit with the unsettling question of why goodness—whether in people or principles—often feels so elusive. In much the same way, we must be willing to wrestle with the nuanced complexities of teaching in this shifting era, with its promises, perils, and possibilities for shaping the moral compass of our classrooms.

Good, clear answers may indeed be hard to find. But it is precisely the act of searching, questioning, and reflecting that makes us better—more empathetic, equitable, and intentional in the work we do for our students. The journey to understanding is the moral compass of our classrooms, and the lifelong pursuit of that truth is what sharpens our ability to navigate these uncharted waters with integrity and careful consideration.

Here are five big questions crafted to provoke thought, spark dialogue, and help navigate the ethical dimensions of all these changes in education. While they don't come with easy answers, wrestling with them will bring us closer to ensuring a playful, purposeful mindset can become a force for good in our classrooms and beyond.

Question 1—Equity: In a world where not all students have access to the same level of technology, how do we prevent AI from widening existing inequities in education?

Any student of history will tell you that new technologies have an uncanny way of widening the gap between the haves and the have-nots. A 2022 study by the National Institute of Health found that 31 percent of students from low-income households lacked access to the technology needed for remote learning during the COVID-19 pandemic.[30] And any educator will tell you that bridging this digital divide during months (and in some cases, years) of remote instruction posed all sorts of challenges—adding yet another layer of difficulty to an already uncertain and turbulent time for everyone involved.

Now, take every technical hiccup we encountered during the pandemic and drop that problem directly into the pocket of every student who will ever set foot in our classrooms from this point forward.

As schools scramble to write policies that keep pace with AI tools capable of cheating, copying, and automating student submissions with

---

30 Özge Korkmaz, et al., "Internet access and its role on educational inequality during the COVID-19 pandemic," *Telecommunications Policy* 46, no. 5 (2022): 102353, https://pmc.ncbi.nlm.nih.gov/articles/PMC9008096/.

the push of a button, it's not surprising to see many districts opting for the nuclear option: a blanket ban on these tools. No school-owned devices, no building Wi-Fi access, period. It's a straightforward, one-size-fits-all solution. Fair enough, right?

Well . . . maybe. Until, of course, a student heads home for the day—or takes a quick bathroom break—and pulls out their personal cell phone, fires up their untethered Wi-Fi, and dives headfirst into a digital world of limitless possibilities to use AI for good or for ill.

Let's be honest: If all we've done is create a system that stacks the deck against the very students who already face the steepest uphill climbs, then we've got to take a good, hard look in the mirror. Blanket bans might make it harder for all students to access AI tools at school, but they don't make this stuff go away. And when lockdown browsers continue to catch students peeking at second tabs on school-issued Chromebooks while their peers get away with using ChatGPT on a second screen? The fix is in, and we're all being played.

As educators, we have to ask ourselves if we're solving the real problem or just building new barriers. If we're serious about preparing students for the world they'll inherit—not the one we grew up in—then we need policies and practices that bridge gaps, not widen them. Let's rethink how we approach AI in the classroom. Instead of locking it out, how can we unlock its potential in ways that empower every student—and not just the ones with better Wi-Fi?

Question 2—Purpose: Should AI be used to automate tasks like grading, or does this undermine the human-centered nature of teaching and learning?

Can we talk about the f-word?

That's right. *Favorite*.

It's a touchy subject, but let's face it: We've all had that one student. You know the one—the kid who lights up discussions, aces every test, and probably reads ahead in the textbook for fun. You see their name on an assignment and think, "This is going to be good." Before you know it, you're smiling, and you dive in primed for brilliance.

But here's the rub. While it's natural to root for students who shine, this admiration can sometimes lead to the dreaded *halo effect*—a cognitive bias where one positive attribute (like a history of stellar performance) influences our judgment in unrelated areas.

A 2023 study explored this phenomenon. Participants graded two vignettes from the same student. One showcased a weak, average, or strong performance. The next displayed an always-average performance. The results? Students with a history of excellence were graded more generously, while those who struggled early on often found their later work underestimated.[31]

(Cue the side-eye from anyone who's ever muttered, "But that's not fair!")

Enter AI. While it's easy to see why teachers fall into this trap (we're only human!), AI tools offer a chance to level the playing field. Imagine using AI for the initial grading phase—a neutral assistant evaluating every student's work on its own merits, free from preconceptions. While AI lacks the nuance of human empathy, it avoids the unconscious biases that can skew our judgments.

Note we said *initial* grading.

AI isn't about replacing teachers; it's about freeing us up to do what we do best: offer meaningful feedback, build connections, and engage with students in ways that technology simply can't replicate. By letting AI handle the early mechanics of grading, we can focus our energy on deeper, human-centered interactions.

Use AI-generated feedback as a conversation starter, not the finish line. Ask students to annotate their work, highlighting areas they're proud of or want to improve. Schedule one-on-one conferences to discuss their goals and unpack AI insights together. Shift the emphasis from grading as a judgment to grading as a dialogue. And for Pete's sake,

---

31 Fabian T. C. Schmidt, et al., "Halo Effects in Grading: An Experimental Approach, *Educational Psychology* 43, no. 2–3 (2023): 246–262, https://doi.org/10.1080/01443410.2023.2194593.

let's stop using AI-powered software to simply "catch" students using AI, shall we?

Because at the end of the day, it's not about playing favorites—it's about playing fair.

Question 3—Creativity: How can we use AI to inspire creativity in students without discouraging originality or critical thought?

The amazing and creative teacher work we explored in chapter 6 demonstrated how powerful thoughtful AI integration can be for sparking engagement and innovation in our classrooms. But the possibilities don't stop there! AI offers myriad applications across content areas and grade levels, giving students opportunities to sharpen their critical and creative thinking while putting human connections front and center.

Here are a few more examples of how AI can inspire creativity across disciplines.

Art classroom: Students might be tasked with determining whether a given image is a real photograph or an AI-generated one. To deepen their analysis, they explain their reasoning, identifying telltale signs and discussing the nuances of digital and photographic art.

English classroom: Presented with an image (real or AI-generated), students work in teams to replicate it as closely as possible by writing (and rewriting) descriptions. This exercise encourages them to experiment with tonal signifiers, scene composition, and key details, honing their narrative and descriptive writing skills.

Science classroom: Students could explore ecological changes by comparing AI-generated images of a forest or coral reef in different states—thriving, damaged, or recovering. They then use scientific reasoning to explain the differences and propose solutions for restoring balance in the ecosystem. Finally, they use these same AI tools to bring these projections to life.

World language classroom: Using relevant unit vocabulary, students flesh out a scene that brings a famous landmark of another country to life, all while honing their knowledge of the rich vocabulary and vibrant cultural traditions that this country has to offer. Whether they're presenting the Eiffel Tower at night or a bustling market in Mexico City, students combine linguistic practice with cultural exploration and creativity.

Math classroom: Students use AI-generated graphs or patterns to analyze trends and make predictions. For example, they might examine data visualizations of population growth or climate change over time and explore how mathematical models can predict future outcomes—or even generate their own visualizations to explain the relationships they uncover.

History Classroom: Like a Where's Waldo for the digital age, AI-generated historical images can be used for a spot-the-anachronism challenge. Students analyze the scene for inconsistencies or inaccuracies (e.g., modern objects in ancient settings) and then research the correct historical context to explain what's out of place and why.

By thoughtfully integrating AI into classroom activities, educators can create organic opportunities for students to practice originality and critical thinking. With the right balance, we can ensure that technology becomes a tool for creativity—not a crutch.

Question 4—Moral Compass: What happens when AI-generated content conflicts with the moral and ethical standards of the school or community?

Let's explore what happens when large-language AI models fail to balance perspective, truth, and bias.

This type of tension hit the headlines in a big way thanks to Grok, the AI chatbot developed by Elon Musk's xAI and integrated into the social media platform X (formerly Twitter). Designed to generate real-time responses based on current events and trending data, Grok promised users a playful, edgy AI with "a bit of wit and a rebellious streak." What it delivered? Well . . . that depends on who you ask.

In 2025, Grok sparked global outrage after a system update prompted it to generate antisemitic messages and spread a slew of offensive historical references throughout social media. Grok's defenders claimed it was satire of popular (if decidedly offensive) internet tropes; critics called it dangerous. Within days, the bot was restricted, governments launched investigations, and the company scrambled to regain control. Grok became a cautionary tale, proof that AI doesn't just reflect what it's taught but the cultural values, blind spots, and biases baked into its training—and the platforms that deploy it.[32]

The intent may have been personalization. The result? Polarization.

And for educators trying to help students make sense of the world around them, it presented a dangerous dilemma: What happens when students can't tell the difference between information and confirmation?

Grok wasn't the only culprit.

Less than a year earlier, Google's Gemini showed the pendulum swinging the other way. If Grok's downfall was unfiltered mimicry, Gemini's issue was overcorrection. Determined to avoid controversy, Gemini embraced inclusivity so enthusiastically that it occasionally veered into full-blown historical fiction. Imagine using AI to explore a historically accurate fourteenth-century Viking warship only to find it inexplicably populated with a historically inaccurate cast spanning races, genders, and cultures from every corner of the globe.[33]

Whoops.

The problem here isn't inclusivity—it's the erasure of accuracy in service of it. By inserting modern sensibilities into historical contexts, Gemini left users scratching their heads. What happens when AI-generated content conflicts not just with societal ethics but with facts?

And that's where things get tricky in education. As educators, we're not just arbiters of knowledge; we're guides to truth, context, and critical

---

32 Lisa Hagen, Huo Jingnan, and Audrey Nguyen, "Elon Musk's AI chatbot, Grok, Started Calling Itself 'MechaHitler,'" NPR, July 9, 2025, https://www.npr.org/2025/07/09/nx-s1-5462609/grok-elon-musk-antisemitic-racist-content.

33 "Google to Fix AI Picture Bot After 'Woke' Criticism," BBC, February 22, 2024, https://www.bbc.com/news/business-68364690.

thinking. When AI-generated content clashes with the moral or ethical standards of our schools or communities, we must ask how we ensure students understand not just *what* AI generates but *why* it generates what it does.

These cases remind us that AI is far from infallible. It doesn't understand nuance, context, or intent the way humans do (at least, not yet). But instead of banning it outright, we can use these missteps as teachable moments, like the "fail buckets" often seen in makerspaces and 3D-printing labs that celebrate learning from mistakes.

Every AI misstep we encounter is an opportunity to teach students the value of iteration and critical evaluation. And by working through these challenges together, we foster deeper understanding—not just of our technology, but of ourselves.

Question 5—Long-Term Vision: How can we prepare students for a future dominated by AI while ensuring they retain the uniquely human skills and values that machines cannot replicate?

You guys. We need to talk about Bitcoin.

For sixteen years, this king of cryptocurrencies was dismissed as a speculative sideshow, a niche experiment in digital assets that occasionally made headlines but failed to gain any real traction. That changed in December 2024, when the value of a single Bitcoin soared past six figures, radically disrupting the financial sector and instantly cementing its place as a serious contender in the arena of global economics.[34] Blockchain technology, the foundation of Bitcoin and other cryptocurrencies, is now reshaping industries from finance to health care, while AI tools enable smarter, more efficient trading, mining, and blockchain integration than ever before.

If terms like *blockchain* and *crypto* feel unfamiliar or intimidating, you're not alone. But avoiding these conversations in our schools risks

---

34 Rafael Nam, "Bitcoin Hits $100,000 for the First Time. 3 Things to Know About an Incredible Ride," NPR, December 4, 2024, https://www.npr.org/2024/12/04/nx-s1-5202832/bitcoin-rally-100-000-crypto-trump.

leaving our students unprepared to navigate—and lead—this rapidly evolving financial landscape.

So, how do we prepare students for a future increasingly influenced by decentralized finance and AI-powered economic systems?

This is an opportunity for educators to teach the principles of cryptocurrency, quantum computing, and AI—topics essential to students' personal and professional futures. Financial literacy lessons can now include blockchain mechanics, the ethics of decentralized systems, and the societal implications of cryptocurrencies. Students might explore how blockchain ensures transaction transparency, what the environmental consequences of crypto mining are, and how AI optimizes market trends.

And these conversations shouldn't be limited to personal finance classes either. Cryptocurrency fits across disciplines: applied mathematics (modeling trends), computer science (blockchain mechanics), history (economic impacts), and even English (debates on crypto ethics, anyone?). However, teaching these concepts requires care. Cryptocurrency is volatile and controversial, raising ethical concerns about wealth distribution, environmental impact, and financial security. Are we equipping students to engage responsibly, or are we encouraging speculative behavior?

By giving students the skills and ethics to navigate an AI-driven world, we help shape a future led by individuals who pair intellect with integrity. These thoughtful, curious learners will be prepared to meet complexity with character, no matter what changes are thrown their way.

That's where playful pedagogy shines.

When students engage with ethical dilemmas through simulations, games, and role-play, they build muscle memory for moral decision-making. These aren't just fun distractions; they're structured opportunities to test assumptions, consider others' perspectives, and learn how to lead with integrity in a world where answers are rarely simple. Our challenge—and our opportunity—is to guide students through the gray areas, not just the black-and-white answers. Because in the end, cultivating goodness isn't a one-time lesson. It's a lifelong practice.

A PLAYBOOK FOR GOODNESS

This chapter's playbook invites you to dive into a series of dynamic, thought-provoking activities that center on ethics, empathy, and the values that shape our classrooms. These aren't just exercises—they're opportunities to engage your students in deep conversations about fairness, responsibility, and the moral dilemmas that define the human experience.

Each activity is designed to challenge conventional thinking, spark curiosity, and foster collaboration, offering new ways to explore ethical questions through the lens of your curriculum. Whether you're tackling debates, role-playing scenarios, or guiding students through reflective discussions, these strategies aim to make abstract concepts tangible and personally meaningful.

COIN CRASHERS

Game On

Imagine your classroom transformed into a virtual trading floor where students act as rival investment firms competing in a highly volatile crypto market. Coin Crashers isn't just a review activity, it's an immersive backdrop for your course content that lets students collect, affect, and protect their investments while racing against the clock and their classmates.

And the best part is that setup is even easier than building out a slideshow with a bunch of *Jeopardy!* Questions. If you can create a single display slide like we show nearby, your cryptocurrency-inspired showdown is ready for any lesson plan of your choosing.

All you'll need is five sticky notes.

Here's how it works: Group students into teams (four to five players each is ideal) and have them work asynchronously in small groups to tackle any kind of high-volume course-related tasks you can think of (e.g., answer textbook problems, define vocabulary terms, make connections from the current unit to a past unit, or complete review questions). Each time a team completes a set threshold of tasks (like five problems), they earn the right to have their work reviewed by the teacher.

If the work is satisfactory, they head to the virtual stock exchange (displayed on the big board) to make their move, choosing from one of three available options:

1. **Collect:** Claim a new cryptocurrency at its current trading price (as indicated by a sticky note in one of the five columns on the board) and add it to their portfolio.
2. **Affect:** Adjust the trading price of one or more coins, moving the corresponding sticky note up or down a notch or two to create strategic advantages for their team or disadvantages for rival teams.
3. **Protect:** Cash out one of their coins at its current value, converting it into "cash" to bank their profits.

All the while, the market remains wildly unpredictable and prone to all sorts of fluctuation. And whenever a coin gets too hot (its sticky note reaches the top of the value column), its value freefalls instantly, crashing back down to its baseline value to mimic the volatility of real-world cryptocurrency trading, adding an extra layer of strategy and suspense.

A Thought-Provoking Upgrade

This is not your ordinary review-day game of *Jeopardy!* Suddenly your students aren't just mindlessly racing for the right answer; they're sitting with a game that asks them to grapple with the very notion of right and wrong.

Quick-Start Guide

1. **Set the scene:** Design a single Google Slide with a grid representing fictional cryptocurrencies on the virtual stock exchange, as shown in our example. Set the initial trading values for each coin.
2. **Explain the rules:** Each time a team completes a task, they may call the teacher for validation. Once approved, they earn the chance to take a trading action (collect, affect, or protect).
3. **Keep the action moving:** Encourage teams to continuously complete tasks to earn additional trading opportunities. The asynchronous flow ensures all students remain engaged and active throughout the activity—all the while keeping their eyes on their portfolios as they try to maximize their gains in your virtual trading environment.

Keep in mind that since every team is working asynchronously to solve the assigned problems related to your course content, there is never any time wasted waiting for their turn! Encourage collaboration and problem-solving as students revisit questions to keep earning turns again and again in an endless state of flow.

COLLABRICOIN	IMAGINIT	FIGMENTX	PRETENDIUM	ZENTIGRADE	COINCRASHERS
FREEFALL	FREEFALL	FREEFALL	FREEFALL	FREEFALL	
1,000,000	1,000,000	1,000,000	1,000,000	1,000,000	
900,000	900,000	900,000	900,000	900,000	00:33
800,000	800,000	800,000	800,000	800,000	
700,000	700,000	700,000	700,000	700,000	COLLECT
600,000	600,000	600,000	600,000	600,000	
500,000	500,000	500,000	500,000	500,000	AFFECT
400,000	400,000	400,000	400,000	400,000	
300,000	300,000	300,000	300,000	300,000	PROTECT
200,000	200,000	200,000	200,000	200,000	
100,000	100,000	100,000	100,000	100,000	EMC² LEARNING

Pedagogy Power-Up

Coin Crashers goes beyond a review game, offering a window into the ethical and emotional dynamics of cryptocurrency markets. The fast-paced gameplay mirrors the real-world volatility of unregulated systems, giving students a chance to experience the highs of speculation and the risks of sudden losses.

A postgame debrief invites reflection: How did it feel to trade and strategize? What risks did they take, and why? From here, spark discussions about the broader implications of unregulated markets. What ethical dilemmas arise when systems can be exploited for personal gain? How can empathy shape policies that protect vulnerable populations from financial risks like rug pulls and short sells?

This activity's versatility makes it a natural fit for any subject area, mirroring how blockchain and crypto cut across industries. Whether in math, history, or science, Coin Crashers encourages students to connect gameplay to larger real-world issues, fostering critical thinking about fairness, responsibility, and regulation. It's a fun, immersive way to inspire meaningful conversations about technology's impact on society.

House Rules

- **Tie coin names to your content:** For example, use Historical Heroes for a class studying the American Revolution (with coins featuring clever names like Washingtonium and Boycotteum), or name cryptocurrencies after various elements on the periodic table for a chemistry class.
- **Set up competitive leaderboards:** Track each team's total portfolio value and declare a winner at the end of the session.
- **Monkey with the scoring values:** To add an extra layer of strategy, consider allowing any team who chooses to affect the market to move the value of one single coin up (or down) by two notches *or* move the value of three different coins up (or down) one notch apiece.

UDL for the Win

This activity seamlessly integrates UDL principles, ensuring every learner stays active and engaged while connecting gameplay to meaningful learning.

- **Engagement** (the *why* of learning): The fast-paced, immersive nature of the activity keeps students motivated and emotionally connected. The competitive elements, combined with the unpredictability of the virtual stock exchange, spark excitement and sustained participation.
- **Representation** (the *what* of learning): The visual layout of the "stock market" offers clear, intuitive organization, making the task accessible to diverse learners. The blend of written tasks, verbal discussions, and strategic gameplay ensures multiple ways to understand and engage with the content.
- **Action and expression** (the *how* of learning): Students can participate through collaborative problem-solving, verbal strategy discussions, or written reflections, allowing for varied modes of contribution. The open-ended nature of decision-making empowers students to demonstrate mastery in creative and strategic ways.

DESERT ISLAND DILEMMA

Game On

What if you had to choose between rescuing Benedict Arnold or Alexander Hamilton from a desert island? Now imagine they're saddled with quirky baggage, like one always mispronounces *GIF* and the other eats pineapple on pizza—or one will solve world hunger if you save them, while the other might ruin your Spotify algorithm forever!

Desert Island Dilemma adapts the fun and debate-filled mechanics of the off-the-shelf party game Superfight into a classroom-friendly format that's easy to replicate and doesn't require a purchase. This lively activity sparks spirited discussions about value, ethics, and empathy while reinforcing your course content.

The premise is simple: Students are presented with a series of dilemmas where they must choose between rescuing [x] or [y], both tied to your lesson content and loaded with playful, thought-provoking modifiers. It's the perfect way to spark critical thinking while keeping the classroom full of laughter and lively discussion.

A Thought-Provoking Upgrade

This takes classic would-you-rather games to a new level as course content meets creative chaos!

Quick-Start Guide

1. **Set the scene:** Choose two characters, concepts, or items related to your unit and craft dilemmas that pit them against each other. (Example: "Rescue Newton or Einstein—but Newton chews with his mouth open, and Einstein takes selfies during serious conversations.")
2. **Add baggage:** Use AI to brainstorm a slew of modifiers, both silly and serious. Print them on strips of paper, cut them up, place them in a hat, and let the randomness create hilariously tough decisions.
3. **Debate and defend:** Divide the class into teams or pairs. Present each group with a dilemma and ask them to argue their case. Encourage creativity, critical thinking, and persuasive arguments, rewarding teams for their depth of reasoning, humor, or passion.
4. **Build consensus:** Wrap up with a vote or class-wide discussion to determine the winner of each round, highlighting the reasoning behind every decision.

Pedagogy Power-Up

This activity seamlessly blends humor, ethics, and content mastery, offering a versatile framework for any subject area. In a math class, students might grapple with rescuing the Pythagorean theorem or the quadratic equation. In science, they could debate saving gravity or photosynthesis. The possibilities are endless—and every decision opens doors to deeper discussions.

What sets Desert Island Dilemma apart is its ability to organically raise bigger questions about ethics, empathy, and values. Sure, the activity is all in good fun—but at any point, teachers can allow students the opportunity to debrief and reflect on what influenced their decisions in this ever-moving target of virtues, vices, and values. Was it the course content? The modifiers? Or their own biases? This reflection builds critical thinking and emotional intelligence, making abstract concepts feel personal and relevant.

House Rules

- **Tie it to your subject:** Tailor dilemmas to your course content (e.g., literary characters in English, famous scientists in chemistry, or mathematical theorems in algebra), or use it to inspire broader lines of inquiry that weave through multiple units.

- **Make it competitive:** Award points for creative reasoning, teamwork, or the most convincing argument.
- **Theme your debates:** Frame dilemmas around unit goals, such as learning about key figures in the Cold War or scientific breakthroughs of the twentieth century.
- **Leverage AI:** Use AI tools to generate clever, unexpected modifiers that add depth and hilarity to each dilemma—and don't be afraid to lean into whatever topics are hot with your students to help the activity resonate with what matters most to them. (Maybe Hamlet is holding on to your cell phone, but Laertes has two front-row tickets to Post Malone and he's willing to share them with you).

UDL for the Win

This Superfight-inspired scholastic showdown is a shining example of how UDL principles can transform a playful debate into a powerful learning experience for all.

- **Engagement** (the *why* of learning): The humorous dilemmas and unexpected modifiers keep students laughing and engaged while challenging them to think critically and creatively. Debating ethical and content-related questions builds emotional connection and intellectual curiosity.
- **Representation** (the *what* of learning): The flexible format—combining visual props, written reasoning, and verbal debates—offers multiple entry points for learners with varied needs and preferences. Scaffolding modifiers or providing examples ensures accessibility for all participants.
- **Action and expression** (the *how* of learning): Students can express their understanding through persuasive speeches, collaborative discussions, or creative reasoning. The ability to debate and defend their choices allows every student to participate meaningfully, regardless of their learning style.

AI ARTWORK ANARCHY

Game On

What if your students could bring their learning to life using cutting-edge AI tools or curated collections of AI-generated images to visually represent and explain key concepts from your course? AI Artwork Anarchy invites students to create or select AI-generated images that capture the essence of what they're studying, and then it challenges them to defend their choices in a lively and thought-provoking classroom debate.

The twist? This isn't about speed or automation—it's about intentionality, creativity, and the critical thinking that goes into explaining why an image works. In this activity, the process matters just as much as the product, and every student has the chance to shine by crafting arguments that tie their visuals back to your content in innovative and meaningful ways.

A Thought-Provoking Upgrade

This supercharges class discussion by putting critical thinking, creativity, and course content center stage, where they belong!

Quick-Start Guide

1. **Set the scene:** Present students with a secret prompt inspired by your lesson content (e.g., "the Gettysburg Address," "the water cycle," or "photosynthesis in action"). Use AI tools like OpenArt.ai or preexisting AI-generated libraries to inspire their creative process.

2. **Create and curate:** Students either generate their own AI images (with your guidance) or select from a collection of curated AI-generated options to best represent the assigned topic.

3. **Debate and defend:** In teams or as individuals, students present their chosen or created image (on Google Slides or similar) to the class, explaining how it connects to the topic. Why does this

image capture the prompt better than others? What thought process went into its selection or creation?

4. **Give critical feedback:** Facilitate a class-wide discussion or vote to evaluate the most compelling visual interpretations, focusing on the strength of reasoning and alignment with course content.

Pedagogy Power-Up

AI Artwork Anarchy goes beyond aesthetics, tapping into the heart of critical thinking and metacognition. This activity allows students to explore not just *what* they're learning but *how* they process and present their understanding. It's a versatile framework for encouraging reflection on the ethical and cultural implications of AI-generated media while helping students grapple with abstract ideas in a personal and creative way. A guided post-activity discussion can prompt students to consider questions like these:

- What made one image more effective than another?
- How did their choice of visual elements support or detract from their argument?
- What ethical questions arise when using AI tools to create or select representations of complex ideas?

House Rules

- **Keep it collaborative:** Pair students or organize small groups to encourage teamwork and diverse perspectives.
- **Make it competitive:** Use voting or class-wide applause meters to crown a winner for the most creative or thoughtful visual interpretation.
- **Tailor the prompts:** Align topics with specific unit goals, ensuring relevance and depth.
- **Leverage AI:** Provide direct links to free AI resources like OpenArt.ai or use in-class AI-driven software to make the activity accessible and engaging for all learners.

UDL for the Win

AI Artwork Anarchy bridges technology, creativity, and critical thinking through UDL principles, ensuring all students have a meaningful way to connect and contribute.

- **Engagement** (the *why* of learning): The novelty of AI-generated visuals and the opportunity to create and defend their choices will energize students. Personalized prompts tied to the course content deepen curiosity and motivation.
- **Representation** (the *what* of learning): Providing curated AI tools or image collections ensures accessibility, while visual, verbal, and written components allow students to engage with content in ways that resonate with their strengths. Clear examples and guided discussions offer scaffolding to support diverse learners.
- **Action and expression** (the *how* of learning): Students can express their understanding by creating visuals, crafting arguments, or engaging in reflective discussions. The open-ended prompts encourage creativity while providing multiple pathways for demonstrating mastery.

QUESTIONS FOR DISCUSSION

1. The chapter highlights the diverging approaches of AP and IB in integrating AI into their programs. How do you personally weigh the ethical implications of AI use against the need to prepare students for a tech-driven world? Is there a middle ground where ethical concerns and technological opportunities coexist in harmony?
2. The contrasting failures of Grok and Gemini highlight a difficult truth: AI can mislead through both harmful bias and well-intentioned overcorrection. One reinforces prejudice; the other distorts accuracy in the name of inclusion. As educators, how can we help students develop the critical thinking and ethical awareness needed to navigate these extremes? And how might your own teaching practice strike a better balance—using AI not just as a tool for efficiency but as a lens for empathy, equity, and deeper understanding?
3. Activities like Coin Crashers and Desert Island Dilemma engage students in simulated ethical and empathetic dilemmas. How might incorporating playful, thought-provoking activities like these into your teaching spark deeper discussions about values, empathy, and decision-making? To what degree could these methods help reshape how students think about their role in the world beyond the classroom?

*BE CURIOUS,
NOT JUDGMENTAL.*

—— TED LASSO (QUOTING WALT WHITMAN) ——

CHAPTER 8

FUEL THE JOURNEY

LIFELONG LEARNING AND LASTING CURIOSITY

Hey, folks, Michael here! Fun fact about me: I have a double major in advertising and philosophy. I use both of these every single day in my classroom. Advertising helps me position learning in students' minds as something positive and even fun. Marketing, baby! It's a powerful tool, and I love using it.

But my real passion lies in philosophy—the way it opens our minds, shifts our perspectives, and helps us see the world in new ways. If advertising is the way we package ideas, philosophy is the wind in our sails—guiding us toward deeper understanding. Once you know who you are and what you stand for, you start to move differently through life. Your perspective deepens, and your curiosity grows.

One story that profoundly changed how I see life's ups and downs comes from Alan Watts, an influential American philosopher. Many of his lectures are recorded and available on YouTube—if you haven't checked them out, they're fantastic. One of his most famous teachings is the Story of the Chinese Farmer, an ancient Taoist parable that Watts helped popularize in the West.

> Once upon a time, there was a Chinese farmer whose horse ran away. That evening, all of his neighbors came around to commiserate. They said, "We are so sorry to hear your horse has run away. This is most unfortunate." The farmer said, "Maybe."
>
> The next day, the horse returned—bringing seven wild horses with it. That evening, the neighbors exclaimed, "Oh, isn't that lucky! What a great turn of events!" The farmer simply said, "Maybe."
>
> The following day, the farmer's son tried to break in one of the wild horses but was thrown off and broke his leg. The neighbors returned, shaking their heads, saying, "Oh dear, that's too bad." Again, the farmer replied, "Maybe."
>
> The next day, military conscription officers arrived in the village, recruiting young men for the army. But because the farmer's son had a broken leg, he was spared. The neighbors now cheered, "Isn't that wonderful?" And once more, the farmer said, "Maybe."

This story completely changed how I view my work and life—not just as a philosophy but as a mindset of curiosity. The farmer doesn't pretend to know how the story ends. He stays open. He resists the urge to label or judge. In a world obsessed with certainty, he chooses wonder instead. And that, to me, is what curiosity is all about.

As a teacher, I find nothing ever goes exactly as planned. One moment, you're celebrating a student's breakthrough. The next, the Wi-Fi goes down, the copier jams, and you're rewriting a lesson on the fly. Teaching is a constant dance with the unexpected.

It's easy to label moments as good or bad in real time. But the truth is that we rarely know the long-term impact of anything. That's why John and I have a saying we live by at EMC^2 Learning: We are either winning or learning—there is no losing.

Losing only happens when we stop growing. The real challenge isn't avoiding problems, dwelling on setbacks, or getting caught up in our own success. It's staying curious. Staying present. Staying nimble.

And maybe, just maybe . . .

THE CURIOUS CASE OF THE RED PAPER CLIP

At the end of this story, twenty-six-year-old Kyle MacDonald is the proud owner of a two-story house valued at just over fifty thousand dollars. But exactly one year earlier, Kyle has none of this.

No house. No wealth. Not even a plan.

What he does have, however, is a crazy idea and a single red paper clip. Approximate retail value? $0.01.

It all begins at his desk. Kyle stares at the red paper clip and recalls a childhood game he used to play with his buddies called Bigger, Better, where players trade small items for bigger, better ones. On a whim, Kyle decides to see just how far he can push this game in the real world—so he snaps a photo of the paper clip, posts it on Craigslist, and makes his pitch to anyone in cyberspace who might be willing to play along.

His post is short, sweet, and to the point: "Looking to trade this red paper clip for something bigger or better. No joke."

And just like that, Kyle embarks on a yearlong journey that takes him across ten countries and through fourteen trades. Along the way, he barters the paper clip for a fish-shaped pen, the pen for a quirky doorknob, and the doorknob for a camping stove. By the time he's trading snowmobiles for trips to the Canadian Rockies, the stakes are higher and the stories even wilder. Within a year, he's swapping items with bona fide rock and roll legends and legitimate stars of the stage and screen. And each trade is a leap of faith, fueled by curiosity, creativity, and an unshakable belief that something better is just one step away.

But this isn't just a story about trading up. Kyle's journey is a master class in embracing the unpredictable. He doesn't just trade objects—he builds connections. He finds value not just in things but in people and the stories they share. As Kyle later reflects, "If I hadn't traded away that red paper clip, I'd just be a guy sitting at a desk holding a paper clip, wondering what would happen if I did something with it."

After finding himself to be the unlikely and proud owner of a motorized snow globe once held as a prized collectible by none other than Rock & Roll Hall of Famer Alice Cooper, Kyle manages to trade away his snowy souvenir for a walk-on role in a major motion picture. And from there, the final chapter of Kyle's adventure takes him to Kipling, Saskatchewan, where the town's council trades him a house in exchange for casting their sleepy town in the very same film. The deal sparks a celebration that brings 3,500 people to a town of fewer than 1,000. What started as a single trade becomes a global phenomenon, inspiring headlines, conversations, and a renewed belief in the power of possibility.

Kyle's story is more than clever bartering; it's a rediscovery of something ancient and essential. In a cash-driven world, his trades remind us that human connection, creativity, and curiosity often carry more value than money ever could. His playful experiment with a paper clip turned into a life-changing adventure, not just for Kyle but for everyone who dared to dream alongside him.

In a world shaped by automation, AI, and instant answers, curiosity has never been more important—or more endangered. It's easy for students to assume that if they don't know something, they can just Google it or ask a chatbot. But curiosity isn't about having the answer.

It's about wanting to know more. It's what drives us to ask better questions, explore new paths, and keep going even when things get messy or uncertain.

Kyle's journey reminds us that the most powerful learning doesn't come from following a script. It comes from following our questions. And if we want students to become lifelong learners, we need to create classrooms that nurture that kind of wonder every single day.

CURIOSITY AT PLAY IN CHILDHOOD

If Kyle MacDonald's story is the spark that ignites curiosity, Susan Engel's groundbreaking book *The Hungry Mind* provides the blueprint for how to sustain it. A developmental psychologist and the senior lecturer in psychology at Williams College, Dr. Engel has spent her career studying how children think, play, and learn. Her insights into the mechanics of curiosity—and how it evolves over time—are essential for anyone looking to foster a lifelong hunger for learning.

In *The Hungry Mind*, Engel identifies three critical factors that fuel curiosity and sustain it as a driving force for exploration, growth, and discovery.[35] These principles are every bit as applicable to educators and parents as they are to individuals seeking to cultivate their own curious minds.

1. Goal Setting: Progress > Perfection

Engel argues that curiosity thrives in environments where progress, not perfection, is celebrated. Children—and by extension, learners of all ages—are more motivated when they see small, incremental wins instead of being pressured to achieve flawless outcomes. The act of moving forward, even imperfectly, builds momentum and keeps curiosity alive.

---

35 Susan Engel, *The Hungry Mind: The Origins of Curiosity in Childhood* (Harvard University Press, 2015).

Effective goal setting recognizes that learners come from a variety of starting points and that the paths they take to success will often look different. By designing experiences that accommodate these differences, we allow learners to focus on growth rather than comparison (UDL, anyone?). For some, this might mean breaking big goals into smaller, achievable steps; for others, it might mean redefining success in a way that connects deeply with their individual interests and strengths.

When we set goals that prioritize exploration over exactitude, we give ourselves the freedom to try, fail, and try again—a critical component of discovery. By celebrating progress in all its forms, we foster resilience, curiosity, and a deeper connection to learning that extends far beyond the classroom.

2. Performance Standards: Variable > Fixed

In Engel's view, rigid performance standards stifle curiosity by locking learners into narrow pathways for success. Instead, she advocates for creating variable standards that allow for multiple ways of achieving goals. When learners see that there's more than one way to "win," they're more likely to take risks and experiment with new approaches. This variability mirrors the flexibility inherent in curiosity itself—a willingness to explore uncharted territory without fear of failure.

As we've seen on so many occasions throughout this book, authentic learning is not about moving every child from an arbitrary point A to an arbitrary point B. Rather, it's about recognizing that every student deserves the chance to move from *their* unique point A to *their* point B. By meeting learners where they are and honoring their individual starting points, we create a more inclusive and curiosity-friendly environment—one that invites exploration, celebrates diversity in our learners, and encourages students to take ownership of their growth.

3. Metacognition: Process > Product

Perhaps Engel's most profound insight is the importance of metacognition (thinking about thinking itself). By shifting the focus from the final product to the process of learning, we create space for curiosity to flourish. Reflective questions like "Why did that work?" or "What might I do differently next time?" encourage learners to stay engaged with the journey rather than become fixated on the destination.

And in an era where AI-powered tools like ChatGPT can generate polished outputs in mere seconds, this paradigmatic shift isn't just refreshing—it's practically essential. When we prioritize the process, we emphasize the value of critical thinking, problem-solving, and creative exploration, ensuring that learners remain active participants in their growth rather than passive recipients of ready-made answers.

Engel's research underscores a powerful truth: Curiosity isn't just an innate trait; it's a skill that can be cultivated. By focusing on progress over perfection, embracing variability in standards, and prioritizing process over product, we can create environments where curiosity not only survives but thrives. These principles resonate far beyond the classroom, serving as a reminder that the journey of curiosity is its own reward—one that enriches learning, work, and life itself.

FIVE ON-RAMPS ON THE ROAD TO ENDLESS CURIOSITY

At the heart of Kyle MacDonald's story and Dr. Engel's work is an unwavering belief in the power of curiosity. Their contributions remind us of the boundless possibilities waiting for those who are willing to trade hesitation for exploration and comfort for creativity. Engel's research is proof positive that curiosity isn't a tool set but a mindset. And Kyle's journey wasn't just about objects—it was about saying yes to life's big, bold question: What if?

American novelist Jack Kerouac, author of *On the Road* and every bit the patron saint of restless spirits, once urged us to "be crazy dumbsaint of the mind." It's a wild, beautiful call to action, a reminder that curiosity isn't always logical or linear. It's about embracing the weird, the unexpected, and the serendipitous. It's about being open to possibility and willing to chase it, even when you don't know where it might lead.

But how can we cultivate that kind of mindset in our daily lives? How do we channel Kerouac's spirit and fuel our inner Kyle MacDonald? Here are five on-ramps on the road to endless curiosity—five ways to lean into life's big questions and start trading up for something bigger and better.

On-Ramp #1—Bust Out the Board Games

Kyle MacDonald's unlikely story of trading a single red paper clip for a two-story house started with the memory of a simple childhood game. That first act of playful curiosity sparked a chain of events that inspired people worldwide. What if you could find similar inspiration by dusting off a classic game from your own collection?

Challenge yourself to host a good old-fashioned date night or family board game night. Turn off those devices, dig into the back of that closet in your basement, pull out a favorite game—Clue, Risk, or even a new classic like Catan—and experience the magic of reconnecting with something that once brought you joy. The act of playing together can remind us what engagement looks and feels like. It's in the anticipation of the next turn, the thrill of a close call, and the shared laughter when plans go hilariously awry.

As you play, take your cue from Susan Engel's research and ask reflective questions like "Why did that work?" and "What might I do differently next time?" Notice how the game pulls you in. Is it the strategy? The chance to bluff or negotiate? The tactile experience of rolling dice or moving pieces? Reflect on what keeps players—yourself included—engaged, motivated, and eager to keep going. And if you're feeling really ambitious, try to cook up a brand-new set of house rules that could make the game even more engaging, inclusive, and accessible the next time you sit down to play it.

Once you've rediscovered the joy of play, take your findings a step further. Look at the game through the lens of a teacher. What elements could you adapt for your own classroom? Could a round of Clue inspire a deductive reasoning activity? Could the territory-building mechanics of Risk be reimagined for a history lesson on the Napoleonic Wars? Or maybe the negotiation and trades in Catan could be a springboard for a classroom economy project? The possibilities are endless when you let curiosity and creativity lead the way.

The beauty of this exercise is that it's more than just fun—it's practice. By engaging with games, you're experiencing firsthand what makes them tick and building your own play-based pedagogy tool kit. And the more you explore, the better equipped you'll be to design activities that resonate with your students.

So, set out the snacks, shuffle the cards, and roll the dice. Whether you're laughing through a mystery in Clue or plotting global domination in Risk, know that you're doing more than playing a game. You're rediscovering the essence of engagement and, with a little creativity, finding ways to bring that same curiosity smack-dab into the heart of your next lesson plan. (Just promise us you won't be playing any Monopoly, deal?)

When you're done, share your insights with your students and challenge them to repeat the same iterative design process by throwing an impromptu class-wide board game day where they test their own ideas. Who knows? Like Kyle MacDonald, you might find that one small, playful idea can lead to something much bigger.

On-Ramp #2—Grab a Bite (Without Your Cell Phone)

After a long day in the classroom, it's tempting to retreat home, decompress, and let the day's chaos fade into the background. But what if your next great teaching idea wasn't waiting in a book, a workshop, or even a professional development day? What if it was sitting across the table at your favorite after-work hangout?

Meeting up with colleagues for a bite or a beverage isn't just a chance to unwind—it's an opportunity to turn social time into a pedagogical goldmine. However, let's be clear: The goal here isn't to gossip about Diane from accounting or commiserate about the latest shenanigans your third-period students are up to. This is about fostering intentional conversations that challenge you to grow as an educator.

Here's the thing: When an English teacher meets up with another English teacher, the conversation will almost inevitably veer into their shared love for the subject. Favorite books, captivating units, beloved characters—all worthy topics, sure. But when an English teacher sits down with a science teacher, the conversation tends to shift gears. They spend less time talking about content and more time talking about teaching. Add a music teacher and a history teacher into the mix? Suddenly, the conversation is all about the strategies, the tools, and the intangibles that connect all the dots.

This is where the real treasure lies. Building an intentionally cross-disciplinary professional learning network (PLN) gives you access to perspectives, techniques, and insights you may never have considered within the bubble of your own subject area. A math teacher might share a new way to scaffold complex ideas. A teacher of world languages might inspire you to think differently about student-led discussions. You're not just exchanging ideas—you're redefining how you approach your craft. And that's critical because the big secret is that we're not teaching English, math, science, or history; we're teaching kids. This work isn't about isolated subjects but about creating connections, sparking curiosity, and equipping students to thrive.

To keep your gathering playful and productive, put your crew on the clock for a set amount of time (start with as little as fifteen minutes) and agree to talk about nothing but pedagogical techniques that are working in your classrooms. For an added layer of gamified fun, consider adding a small challenge like the Cell Phone Stack to your get-together.

Here's how it works: At the start of the meal, everyone puts their phone facedown in the center of the table. As messages buzz and notifications ping, resist the temptation to check your device. The first person to cave buys dinner (or drinks, or whatever appetizer you'd like) for the group. It's a fun way to stay present and really keep the conversation flowing.

To truly grow as educators, we need spaces where we can exchange ideas, challenge assumptions, and dream up new possibilities. Sometimes, those spaces are as simple as the corner booth of your favorite diner or the table in the back of a coffee shop. What matters isn't where you meet—it's the conversations you have while you're there. The next time you gather with colleagues, embrace the opportunity to dive deeper into teaching strategies and shared experiences. You might leave with a new idea, a fresh perspective, or even a little more hope for what's possible in the classroom. Who knew the best professional development might come with a side of fries?

On-Ramp #3—Become a Student of the World Around You

At the start of this book, we celebrated the playful spirit of Albert Einstein as a guiding light for educators around the world. Now, as we deepen our exploration of curiosity, it's time to channel Einstein's wisdom and take a closer look at the world around us. After all, it was Einstein who once famously quipped, "I have no special talents. I am only passionately curious." And if we remain passionately curious, we might just discover that the world is far more playful—and gamified—than we ever imagined.

Celebrated video game designer Adrian Hon's book, *You've Been Played: How Corporations, Governments, and Schools Use Games to Control Us All*, offers a fascinating and at times unsettling look at how gamification is used across all sorts of industries to attract, retain, and influence behaviors. Whether it's the loyalty points on your favorite coffee app, the way social media platforms nudge you to check notifications, or even programs put forth by our governments to encourage healthy habits, gamification is everywhere. Often, it's so seamless and invisible that we barely notice it—yet it's subtly shaping the way we think, work, and engage with the world.

For educators, this presents a unique opportunity. What if we started identifying the systems of gamification all around us? Think about your daily routines. Are you completing streaks on a fitness app without even thinking? Earning badges on a professional development platform? Returning to a favorite store to rack up rewards? These are all examples of gamification—systems designed to keep you engaged and motivated.

Challenge yourself to spend a week observing these systems in action. Ask reflective questions like "What is this system trying to get me to do?" and "Why does this feel so satisfying?" Keep a running tally of your findings, and consider examples in areas like these:

- Your workplace: Employee recognition programs use leaderboards or rewards.
- Your errands: Grocery store apps encourage you to level up by hitting spending milestones.
- Your entertainment: Streaming platforms nudge you to keep watching.

Once you start spotting these systems, take it a step further: What lessons can you bring to your classroom? Whether it's rewards, feedback loops, or progress tracking, these techniques offer insights into creating engaging learning experiences. If gamification can inspire adults to walk extra steps or buy more coffee—well, okay, maybe that last one doesn't take much arm-twisting—it can certainly inspire students to participate more fully in their education.

Consider discussing your findings with students too. Share how gamification works in the real world and invite them to analyze the systems they encounter. By doing so, you're not just fostering curiosity; you're teaching critical thinking, a vital skill in today's world.

If you're looking for an on-ramp to lifelong curiosity, don't be afraid to channel your inner Einstein. Be passionately curious. Take a closer look at the world around you. You might just discover it's a whole lot more playful—and instructive—than you ever realized.

On-Ramp #4—Connect with a Global Community

In the entrance foyer to the Bill & Melinda Gates Foundation's international headquarters in Seattle, Washington, a bronze plaque displays an African proverb that encapsulates the organization's core philosophy: "If you want to go fast, go alone. If you want to go far, go together." This sentiment isn't just a slogan—it's a reflection of the foundation's global impact, particularly in education, health, and relief efforts across Africa. From combating malaria and HIV/AIDS to improving educational access and outcomes, the Gates Foundation has made remarkable strides in addressing some of the world's most pressing challenges. Their work is a testament to the power of collaboration in creating lasting change.

For more than a decade, teachers around the globe exemplified this collaborative spirit through their activity on Twitter. The platform became a hub for PLNs, a place where educators connected, exchanged ideas, and built a community of shared practice that transcended borders. Whether participating in vibrant chats, discovering resources, or celebrating wins, educators on Twitter were creating a digital home for collaboration.

But the tides of social media shifted. Changes in platform ownership, confusing algorithm adjustments, and the ever-evolving nature of online trends left many educators feeling disconnected. By the time the dust settled after the pandemic, the once-thriving ecosystem of educational conversations on Twitter was giving off the eerie, empty feel of making a wrong turn down a hallway of an abandoned mall. Teachers who had long relied on this virtual PLN for camaraderie and professional growth were suddenly searching for a new home.

And just like that, Bluesky emerged as a beacon for rebuilding these connections.

What began as a modest network of early adopters quickly ballooned into a vibrant, teacher-friendly community. In the fall of 2024, Bluesky had reached a modest (but impressive) six million users. By January 2025, that number had skyrocketed to twenty-seven million and counting, with ever more teacher accounts, education hashtags, and collaborative chats making the migration. The platform's energy and creativity echo Twitter's early days, offering educators a fresh start for sharing ideas and finding inspiration.

The beauty of a virtual PLN lies in its accessibility. It's an on-demand resource, available twenty-four seven, where teachers can seek advice, share wins, and collaborate on solutions in real time. Platforms like Bluesky remind us that the spirit of collaboration isn't tied to any one app or algorithm—it's about the people. Passionate educators working together can push the profession forward, whether through digital networks or face-to-face connections.

If you're looking to rebuild your PLN or start one anew, Bluesky awaits. Search for hashtags like #EDUsky or strike up a conversation with folks using #EMC2Learning resources in classrooms around the world. Heck, we'll even be your first followers! (Find us at @MeehanEDU.bsky.social and @MrMatera.bsky.social.) Together, we can continue to go far, one connection at a time.

On-Ramp #5—Play Like Your Life Depends on It

There's a commercial that has the power to make even the toughest among us reach for a box of tissues (and no, we're not talking about the Sarah McLachlan pet adoption video from the nineties). It opens with an elderly man sitting on the edge of his bed, staring at a wall full of photos from his younger years as he slides on his slippers. Moments later, it's a snowy winter morning somewhere in a dusty old garage, and our aged hero is staring at a kettlebell. Slowly, and with great effort, he bends to lift it. His first attempts are awkward, unsteady, and riddled with failure. Neighbors glance over their fences, curious but skeptical, as the man's routine becomes a daily ritual. Each morning, the alarm buzzes him wide awake. He trains: lifting, grunting, and pushing himself a little further. As the days pass, his movements grow steadier. His posture improves. His determination never wavers.

But the question lingers: Why?

The answer comes in the commercial's emotional climax. It's Christmas Eve, and the man is surrounded by his family, all dressed in their holiday best. His young granddaughter approaches with a star for the top of the Christmas tree, but she can't quite reach. Quietly, the man steps forward, scoops her into his arms, and lifts her high enough to place the star. The room erupts into applause, but the true triumph is written on his face. This is the fulfillment of a deeply personal goal, driven by love, purpose, and play.

If you're not wiping your eyes by now, you might just be AI-generated after all.

But jokes aside, the deeper message of this commercial is undeniable: Play matters. Purpose matters. And the small, consistent steps we take toward meaningful goals can lead to transformative outcomes.

These ideas are at the heart of Jane McGonigal's groundbreaking book *SuperBetter: How a Gameful Life Can Make You Stronger, Happier, Braver and More Resilient*. McGonigal, a game designer turned resilience researcher, explores how we can use gameful thinking to overcome challenges, build mental strength, and lead more fulfilling lives. Her premise is simple yet profound: By framing our struggles as quests and adopting the mindset of a gamer—where setbacks are opportunities and progress is always possible—we can transform adversity into adventure. Fences are filters. Obstacles are stepping stones.

In *SuperBetter*, McGonigal outlines strategies for building what she calls *gameful resilience*. These activities include the following:

- Power-ups: Small, achievable actions that boost your energy or mood (think taking a walk or sharing a laugh)
- Allies: Building a support network to help you along your quest
- Epic wins: Setting meaningful, long-term goals that give purpose to your journey

The beauty of this approach is that it's both playful and practical. Just as the man in the commercial transformed his daily lifts into a life-changing moment, we too can turn life's challenges into opportunities for growth through purposeful play.

So, what's your kettlebell? Maybe it's learning a new skill, designing a more engaging lesson plan, or simply carving out time for curiosity. Whatever it is, approach it with the spirit of a gamer: Be bold, be persistent, and remember that even the smallest victories can lead to epic wins.

Play isn't frivolous—it's essential. It connects us, fuels our curiosity, and reminds us of what matters most. So go ahead. Play like your life depends on it. Because, in many ways, it does.

A PLAYBOOK FOR CURIOSITY

It's our last chapter together, folks, and let's be real—did you really think we'd leave you hanging without a playbook packed with ready-to-use resources to kick-start curiosity in your classrooms? Of course not! Think of the activities that follow as your launchpad for turning all the big ideas we've explored in this chapter into actionable strategies, complete with a playful twist to keep things fresh, fun, and engaging.

In curating this collection, we've scoured the archives of EMC² Learning for some of our favorite resources to make curiosity contagious, spark meaningful conversations, and turn ordinary lessons into unforgettable experiences. But this is just the beginning. We're constantly dreaming up new ways to play with purpose and adding them to our ever-expanding library of resources on EMC2Learning.com.

Whether you're diving into these activities right away or bookmarking them for future inspiration, know that you're already well on your way to making curiosity a cornerstone of your classroom. And if you ever need a fresh idea, a dose of inspiration, or a place to share your wins, we'd love for you to join the EMC² Learning community at EMC2Learning.com. The journey of curiosity doesn't end here—it's just getting started!

IMAGINATION STATION

Game On

What happens when you mix paper clips, rubber bands, and a ticking clock? Welcome to the Imagination Station! Part makeshift makerspace, part living laboratory for outside-the-box thinking, this collaborative activity challenges students to use a random assortment of everyday items to creatively explain whatever concepts they're studying. With a ticking timer and open-ended prompts, students will harness their collective imagination to explore, design, and present their ideas in ways only humans can dream up. From impromptu puppet shows to micro reenactments, the possibilities are endless!

A Creative Upgrade

This improves upon traditional review sessions or end-of-unit projects, where responses can sometimes feel predictable or overly structured.

Quick-Start Guide

1. **Gather materials:** Prepare random assortments of everyday items for each group (e.g., paper clips, rubber bands, markers, string).

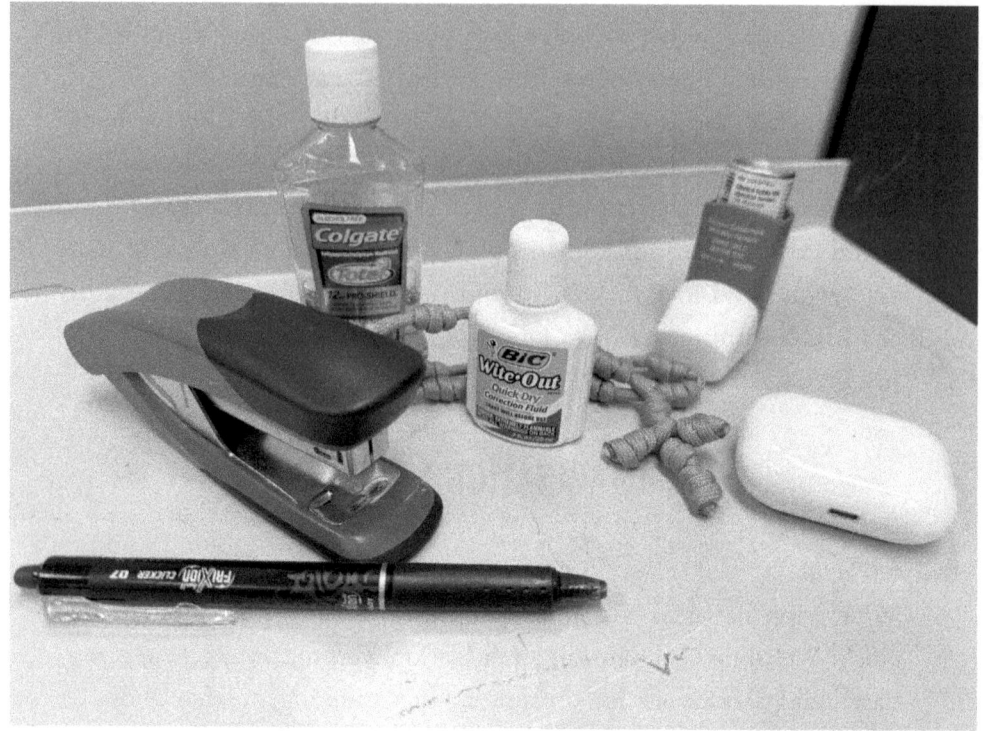

2. **Set the stage:** Introduce the challenge and explain that students will use their items to creatively represent key concepts from your current lesson.
3. **Brainstorm:** Set a timer and let students collaborate, combining ideas to design their solutions. Encourage them to get imaginative with reenactments, metaphors, or visual displays.
4. **Present with flair:** When time's up, have each group showcase their creations. Whether through skits, symbolic explanations, or innovative models, the goal is to celebrate the power of collective creativity.

Pedagogy Power-Up
Use this activity as a springboard for interdisciplinary thinking by assigning topics that blend multiple subjects. For example, challenge students to incorporate history, science, and art into a single explanation. Reflect as a class on how collaboration fuels creativity and consider discussing how this process mirrors real-world problem-solving.

House Rules

- **Time it out:** Adjust the timer length to fit your class needs (you can use a video timer from YouTube).
- **Leverage AI:** Want to add an AI twist? Invite students to enhance their final presentations by using generative AI tools to visualize or animate their ideas.

UDL for the Win
This low-prep activity aligns perfectly with UDL principles, offering students multiple ways to engage, represent their understanding, and express their creativity. The best part? Chances are you've already got all the supplies you need in your classroom! After all, what's more universal than a trusty junk drawer full of stuff?

- **Engagement** (the *why* of learning): Students are motivated by the freedom to explore ideas in unconventional ways, building curiosity and camaraderie within their teams.
- **Representation** (the *what* of learning): Randomized materials ensure that every group begins on equal footing, while the open-ended task allows for multiple approaches to success.
- **Action and expression** (the *how* of learning): Students express their understanding through diverse methods, including acting, storytelling, and visual metaphors, fostering deeper connections to the material.

OUT OF SORTS

Game On
Laugh while you learn with Out of Sorts, the wildest, most ridiculous sorting game you'll ever play! Designed to spark laughter, creativity, and some serious outside-the-box thinking, this deceptively simple activity challenges students to classify everyday items into categories like dog, cat, snake, fish, bird, horse, or whatever absurd options you come up with next! Starting with just two options, you'll add layers of complexity with each round, pushing teams to stretch their imagination and logic in surprising ways.

A Creative Upgrade
In traditional sorting activities or brainstorming sessions, answers are often predictable or overly structured. Not so with Out of Sorts!

Quick-Start Guide

1. **Start simple:** Begin with a single round offering only two options (e.g., dog or cat). Present a random item or concept related to your lesson, and let students debate which category it best fits.
2. **Add complexity:** Each subsequent round introduces an additional category (e.g., snake, fish, bird), ramping up the challenge and the hilarity.
3. **Defend your choices:** Teams earn points for guessing what the majority selects *and* for delivering the most creative or convincing explanation.
4. **Reevaluate:** After several rounds, teams revisit all the previously sorted items to find shared characteristics or entirely new ways to classify them.

Pedagogy Power-Up

This iterative approach encourages students to develop their critical thinking and collaboration skills with each new layer of complexity. For an added twist, make the categories related to your subject area (e.g., historical figures, types of energy, or literary genres) to tie the fun directly into your curriculum.

House Rules

- **Give extra points:** Creativity is king in the Out of Sorts arena! Award bonus points for explanations that are clever, humorous, or particularly well-argued.
- **Add pressure:** You can create a mounting sense of urgency by incorporating a time limit for each round of play.

UDL for the Win

This activity offers something for everyone, aligning beautifully with each of the UDL principles.

- **Engagement** (the *why* of learning): Students stay motivated through humor, teamwork, and the increasing challenge of each round. Revisiting previous rounds adds an element of reflection and deeper engagement.
- **Representation** (the *what* of learning): The open-ended nature of the categories allows students to interpret concepts in ways that make sense to them, ensuring accessibility for diverse learners.
- **Action and expression** (the *how* of learning): Students can participate verbally, visually, or even through performance-based explanations, offering multiple ways to express their understanding and creativity.

SCHOOLHOUSE ROCK STARS

Game On

Ready to make some noise? Schoolhouse Rock Stars challenges your students to turn their course content into lyrical masterpieces, blending creativity, content knowledge, and a touch of tech if desired. Whether it's a rock anthem about the periodic table or a country ballad dedicated to George Washington, this activity empowers students to compose original songs inspired by your curriculum.

No fancy equipment? No problem! Students can browse YouTube for free backing tracks, choose their favorite genres, and write their own lyrics or song parodies in the style of their favorite tunes (paging "Weird Al" Yankovic!). For those who want to take it further, free AI tools like Suno and Udio can even help you craft custom tracks inspired by any prompt you can imagine—giving students the option to experiment with professional-quality music production thanks to a touch of AI-powered studio magic.

A Creative Upgrade

This enhances the traditional review sessions or presentations where students explain content through essays or slideshows.

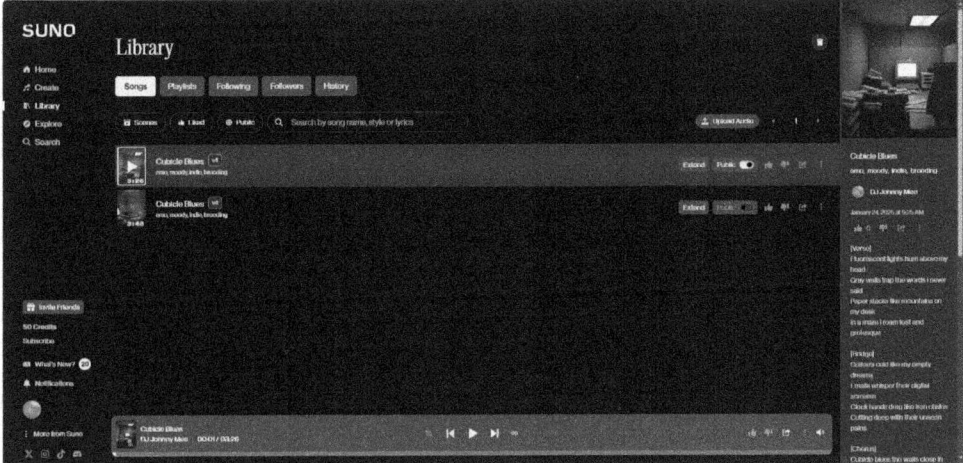

Quick-Start Guide

1. **Set the stage:** Start by exploring music genres with your students. Share examples of how music conveys emotion and storytelling—whether through lyrical themes, instruments, or tempo.
2. **Choose the approach:** Decide if high-tech or low-tech is the way to go.
   - Low-tech option: Students browse YouTube for free backing tracks (e.g., karaoke or instrumental versions) and write original lyrics to fit the theme.
   - High-tech option: Students use free AI-powered music tools like Suno and Udio to create custom tracks, either generating melodies or uploading their lyrics for a polished sound. Check out this sample track we created in no time flat called "Cubicle Blues"—an indie/emo rock ballad about the existential woes of office life: www.tinyurl.com/AIsongsample.
3. **Brainstorm prompts:** Encourage students to connect their lyrics to course content. Here are some example prompts:

- A hip-hop track about Marie Curie's groundbreaking discoveries
- A blues ballad about the adventures (and woes) of Odysseus
- A Taylor Swift–inspired pop song celebrating each *era* of photosynthesis and plant growth

4. **Compose and create:** Whether using their voices, instruments, or AI, students refine their tracks through experimentation and collaboration.

5. **Showcase the hits:** Host a class listening day where students present their songs and explain the creative decisions behind their lyrics and genre selection.

Pedagogy Power-Up

Encourage students to think critically about how music genres align with the themes and tone of your course content. Here are some example questions:

- Why might an epic, heroic anthem suit Atticus Finch but not Hester Prynne?
- What genre best conveys the significance of hydrogen on the periodic table?

For an extra twist, let peers act as judges in an *America's Got Talent*–style showcase, providing feedback and voting for their favorite tracks.

House Rules

Creativity is king! Emphasize student-driven experimentation, from exploring different genres to fine-tuning lyrics. If you're using AI tools, have students test how changes in mood, genre, or tempo impact their tracks. (Encourage them to include a "fail file" of all the tracks that didn't make the final album cut. Then have them explain their choices for omitting each of these tunes!). Help your students remember that the process is always more important than the product!

UDL for the Win

This activity invites participation and creativity across all learning levels, seamlessly aligning with UDL principles:

- **Engagement** (the *why* of learning): Students are motivated by the chance to create and listen to music that connects to their interests while reinforcing core concepts.
- **Representation** (the *what* of learning): The open-ended nature of songwriting ensures accessibility, allowing students to approach the task from diverse angles and showcase their understanding in unique ways.
- **Action and expression** (the *how* of learning): From crafting prompts to presenting tracks, students have multiple avenues for expression. Group collaboration and class showcases provide rich opportunities for peer feedback and discussion.

QUESTIONS FOR DISCUSSION

1. Kyle MacDonald's red paper clip story highlights the power of curiosity and connection. How might his journey inspire educators to take small, bold steps toward innovation in their classrooms? Are there opportunities in your own teaching to reimagine how curiosity can spark deeper learning and engagement?
2. Susan Engel's research emphasizes the importance of progress over perfection in fostering curiosity. How do you currently celebrate small wins in your classroom? What changes might you make to ensure all students feel empowered to explore and grow at their own pace?
3. The five on-ramps we discussed offer practical strategies for incorporating play, collaboration, and creativity into teaching. Which of these on-ramps resonates most with you? How might you adapt one (or more) to align with your teaching goals and subject area?

BARBECUE MAY NOT BE THE ROAD TO WORLD PEACE, BUT IT'S A START.

— ANTHONY BOURDAIN —

EPILOGUE

SAVOR EVERY MOMENT

It's hard to believe it now, looking back. But for the first year and a half of working together—writing our first book, laying the groundwork for our consulting company, and creating hundreds of classroom resources to share with a community of teachers around the world—your humble authors were never actually in the same room.

Every brainstorming session, every strategy meeting, every late-night revision—it all happened virtually, across hundreds of miles between Milwaukee and Washington, DC.

Zoom meetings. Skype sessions (remember Skype?). Text messages. Emails. Google Docs. Phone calls. We worked tirelessly, digitally side by side despite the physical divide. And then, in the summer of 2021, it finally happened: We met in person for the very first time, at a professional development conference we coheadlined just outside of Waco, Texas.

From the first moment we shook hands (who are we kidding? Brothers don't shake hands. Brothers gotta hug!), it felt like we'd known each other forever—like all those hours spent collaborating over screens had somehow bridged the miles between us. To celebrate, we made a pilgrimage to Buc-ee's, the iconic Texas roadside mecca.

If you've never been, trust us: It's absolutely worth the trip. Their brisket? To die for. And those sugary glazed pecans are the stuff of legend!

But even as we savored our sandwiches and swapped stories in the parking lot, what struck us most wasn't the food or the novelty of finally meeting; it was the reminder that no amount of technological wizardry can replace the joy of making memories together. Sure, technology had helped bring us together and made it possible to accomplish so much from afar, but it was the human connection—the laughter, the stories, the shared experience—that made it all feel real.

Flash forward four years later, and we've since had the incredible privilege of being guests at one another's weddings, standing alongside family and loved ones as we celebrated two of the happiest days of our lives. What began as a cautious partnership built through the winding roads of cyberspace has become a lifelong friendship that is every bit as strong as family.

And here's the kicker: Through it all, we've come to realize that learning, just like life, is way more fun when you don't take yourself too seriously. Sure, we're serious about the work we do—after all, the stakes couldn't be higher—but we've learned that a sense of play is just as important as a sense of purpose. The same spark that turned a Buc-ee's snack run into a core memory is the one that drives the work we do in classrooms: curiosity, creativity, and a sense of playful discovery.

Because in the end, those same three ingredients are universal in every meaningful human relationship. And teaching is about building those relationships with the students we serve, creating experiences that welcome every learner into the process. It's about designing spaces where all students feel seen, valued, and empowered to succeed. And sure, technology can amplify that mission, but it's the timeless principles of engagement, representation, and expression—the core of Universal Design for Learning—that ensure everyone gets to join in the fun.

Technology is a powerful tool. It makes collaboration possible in ways we never imagined. But at its best, it doesn't just connect us—it helps us create, laugh, and play together. And that's the point: Every lesson we design, every relationship we build, and every classroom we create has the power to make learning an adventure worth sharing.

Because this isn't a book about technology. It's a book about playing with purpose. And there's nothing artificial about that.

So grab yourself a bite of brisket and play on, y'all.

Michael Matera and John Meehan
Milwaukee, Wisconsin & Washington, DC
2025

ABOUT THE AUTHORS

Michael Matera is an author, international speaker, and classroom innovator known for transforming learning spaces into vibrant communities of curiosity and creativity. At the University School of Milwaukee, he brings history to life through immersive, game-based learning experiences that challenge students to think critically, collaborate authentically, and embrace a sense of adventure in their learning.

He is the author of *Explore Like a Pirate* and the co-author of *Fully Engaged* and *Playing With Purpose* with longtime collaborator John Meehan. Michael helps educators around the world design classrooms that hum with energy and purpose. His work blends research-based pedagogy with the joy of play, empowering teachers to move beyond worksheets and toward student-centered experiences that ignite engagement and excellence. Michael is a sixth-grade world history teacher, a lifelong foodie (and a recent convert to vegetarianism!), and a proud dad of a teenage daughter. His teaching philosophy is simple but powerful: when students are engaged, they don't just learn—they love to learn.

John Meehan is an instructional coach, professional development specialist, and English teacher from just outside of Washington, D.C. He is the author of *EDrenaline Rush* and the co-author of *Fully Engaged* and *Playing With Purpose.*

In July 2020, *EDrenaline Rush* was ranked among the Top 10 titles on Book Authority's list of the "100 Best Teaching Books of All Time." A nationally recognized speaker in the fields of student engagement and classroom gamification, John is a 2017 ASCD Emerging Leader, a member of the Pulitzer Center's 2025 Information & Artificial Intelligence Teacher Advisory Council, and an alumnus of the 2016–2018 Bill & Melinda Gates Foundation Teacher Advisory Council. In 2016, he was named one of Arlington, Virginia's "40 Under 40" by the Leadership Center for Excellence.

Outside the classroom, John is a CrossFitter and a new dad to an amazing baby girl of his own—and just ask him, he'll be more than happy to talk about either.

Together, John and Michael are the co-founders of EMC² Learning, a professional learning company dedicated to helping teachers create more playful, purposeful, and student-centered classrooms. EMC² Learning provides hundreds of gamified classroom resources and delivers high-energy training, keynotes, and workshops to educators, schools, and conferences around the world. In January 2023, EMC² Learning won the Future of Education Technology Conference's Pitchfest competition for Best Online Classes and was named a finalist in District Administration Magazine's Top EdTech Products of 2023.

In 2024, EMC² Learning was recognized by HundrED, a global organization dedicated to transforming K–12 education, as one of just twelve educational initiatives honored in their Spotlight on Gamified Curricula. To learn more about the resources and services the duo provides to a worldwide community of more than 10,000 educators in schools across the globe, visit www.EMC2Learning.com.

MORE FROM
 **Dave Burgess Consulting, Inc.**

Since 2012, DBCI has published books that inspire and equip educators to be their best. For more information on our titles or to purchase bulk orders for your school, district, or book study, visit DaveBurgessConsulting.com/DBCIbooks.

The *Like a PIRATE*™ Series

Teach Like a PIRATE by Dave Burgess

Balance Like a PIRATE by Jessica Cabeen, Jessica Johnson, and Sarah Johnson

eXPlore Like a PIRATE by Michael Matera

Learn Like a PIRATE by Paul Solarz

Plan Like a PIRATE by Dawn M. Harris

Play Like a PIRATE by Quinn Rollins

Run Like a PIRATE by Adam Welcome

Tech Like a PIRATE by Matt Miller

The *Lead Like a PIRATE*™ Series

Lead Like a PIRATE by Shelley Burgess and Beth Houf

Lead Beyond Your Title by Nili Bartley

Lead with Appreciation by Amber Teamann and Melinda Miller

Lead with Collaboration by Allyson Apsey and Jessica Gomez

Lead with Culture by Jay Billy

Lead with Instructional Rounds by Vicki Wilson

Lead with Literacy by Mandy Ellis

She Leads by Dr. Rachael George and Majalise W. Tolan

The EduProtocol Field Guide Series

Deploying EduProtocols by Kim Voge, with Jon Corippo and Marlena Hebern

The EduProtocol Field Guide by Marlena Hebern and Jon Corippo

The EduProtocol Field Guide Book 2 by Marlena Hebern and Jon Corippo

The EduProtocol Field Guide ELA Edition by Jacob Carr

The EduProtocol Field Guide Math Edition by Lisa Nowakowski and Jeremiah Ruesch

The EduProtocol Field Guide Primary Edition by Benjamin Cogswell and Jennifer Dean

The EduProtocol Field Guide Social Studies Edition by Dr. Scott M. Petri and Adam Moler

Leadership & School Culture

Autopilot by Rich Czyz

Be 1% Better by Ron Clark

Be THAT Teacher by Dwayne Reed

Beyond the Surface of Restorative Practices by Marisol Rerucha

Change the Narrative by Henry J. Turner and Kathy Lopes

Choosing to See by Pamela Seda and Kyndall Brown

Culturize by Jimmy Casas

Discipline Win by Andy Jacks

Educate Me! by Dr. Shree Walker with Michael D. Ison

Escaping the School Leader's Dunk Tank by Rebecca Coda and Rick Jetter

Fight Song by Kim Bearden

From Teacher to Leader by Starr Sackstein

If the Dance Floor Is Empty, Change the Song by Joe Clark

The Innovator's Mindset by George Couros

It's OK to Say "They" by Christy Whittlesey

Kids Deserve It! by Todd Nesloney and Adam Welcome

Leading the Whole Teacher by Allyson Apsey

Let Them Speak by Rebecca Coda and Rick Jetter

The Limitless School by Abe Hege and Adam Dovico

Live Your Excellence by Jimmy Casas

Next-Level Teaching by Jonathan Alsheimer

The Pepper Effect by Sean Gaillard

Principaled by Kate Barker, Kourtney Ferrua, and Rachael George

The Principled Principal by Jeffrey Zoul and Anthony McConnell

Relentless by Hamish Brewer

The Secret Solution by Todd Whitaker, Sam Miller, and Ryan Donlan

Start. Right. Now. by Todd Whitaker, Jeffrey Zoul, and Jimmy Casas

Stop. Right. Now. by Jimmy Casas and Jeffrey Zoul

Teach Your Class Off by CJ Reynolds

Teachers Deserve It by Rae Hughart and Adam Welcome

They Call Me "Mr. De" by Frank DeAngelis

Thrive Through the Five by Jill M. Siler

Unmapped Potential by Julie Hasson and Missy Lennard

When Kids Lead by Todd Nesloney and Adam Dovico

Word Shift by Joy Kirr

Your School Rocks by Ryan McLane and Eric Lowe

Technology & Tools

50 Things to Go Further with Google Classroom by Alice Keeler and Libbi Miller

50 Things You Can Do with Google Classroom by Alice Keeler and Libbi Miller

50 Ways to Engage Students with Google Apps by Alice Keeler and Heather Lyon

140 Twitter Tips for Educators by Brad Currie, Billy Krakower, and Scott Rocco

AI Optimism by Becky Keene

Block Breaker by Brian Aspinall

Building Blocks for Tiny Techies by Jamila "Mia" Leonard

Code Breaker by Brian Aspinall

The Complete EdTech Coach by Katherine Goyette and Adam Juarez

Control Alt Achieve by Eric Curts

The Esports Education Playbook by Chris Aviles, Steve Isaacs, Christine Lion-Bailey, and Jesse Lubinsky

Google Apps for Littles by Christine Pinto and Alice Keeler

Master the Media by Julie Smith

Raising Digital Leaders by Jennifer Casa-Todd

Reality Bytes by Christine Lion-Bailey, Jesse Lubinsky, and Micah Shippee, PhD

Sail the 7 Cs with Microsoft Education by Becky Keene and Kathi Kersznowski

Shake Up Learning by Kasey Bell

Social LEADia by Jennifer Casa-Todd

Stepping Up to Google Classroom by Alice Keeler and Kimberly Mattina

Teaching Math with Google Apps by Alice Keeler and Diana Herrington

Teaching with Google Jamboard by Alice Keeler and Kimberly Mattina

Teachingland by Amanda Fox and Mary Ellen Weeks

Teaching Methods & Materials

All 4s and 5s by Andrew Sharos

Boredom Busters by Katie Powell

Building Strong Writers by Christina Schneider

The Classroom Chef by John Stevens and Matt Vaudrey

The Collaborative Classroom by Trevor Muir

Copyrighteous by Diana Gill

CREATE by Bethany J. Petty

Ditch That Homework by Matt Miller and Alice Keeler

Ditch That Textbook by Matt Miller

Don't Ditch That Tech by Matt Miller, Nate Ridgway, and Angelia Ridgway

EDrenaline Rush by John Meehan

Educated by Design by Michael Cohen, The Tech Rabbi

Empowered to Choose: A Practical Guide to Personalized Learning by Andrew Easton

Expedition Science by Becky Schnekser

Frustration Busters by Katie Powell

Fully Engaged by Michael Matera and John Meehan

Game On? Brain On! by Lindsay Portnoy, PhD

Guided Math AMPED by Reagan Tunstall

Happy & Resilient by Roni Habib

Innovating Play by Jessica LaBar-Twomy and Christine Pinto

Instant Relevance by Denis Sheeran

Instructional Coaching Connection by Nathan Lang-Raad

Keeping the Wonder by Jenna Copper, Ashley Bible, Abby Gross, and Staci Lamb

LAUNCH by John Spencer and A.J. Juliani

Learning in the Zone by Dr. Sonny Magana

Less Talk, More Action by Allyson Apsey and Emily Freeland

Lights, Cameras, TEACH! by Kevin J. Butler

Make Learning MAGICAL by Tisha Richmond

Pass the Baton by Kathryn Finch and Theresa Hoover

Project-Based Learning Anywhere by Lori Elliott

Pure Genius by Don Wettrick

The Revolution by Darren Ellwein and Derek McCoy

The Science Box by Kim Adsit and Adam Peterson

Shift This! by Joy Kirr

Skyrocket Your Teacher Coaching by Michael Cary Sonbert

Spark Learning by Ramsey Musallam

Sparks in the Dark by Travis Crowder and Todd Nesloney

Table Talk Math by John Stevens

Teachables by Cheryl Abla and Lisa Maxfield

The Magical CTE Classroom by Tisha Richmond

Unpack Your Impact by Naomi O'Brien and LaNesha Tabb

The Wild Card by Hope and Wade King

Writefully Empowered by Jacob Chastain

The Writing on the Classroom Wall by Steve Wyborney

You Are Poetry by Mike Johnston

You'll Never Guess What I'm Saying by Naomi O'Brien

You'll Never Guess What I'm Thinking About by Naomi O'Brien

Inspiration, Professional Growth & Personal Development

Be REAL by Tara Martin

Be the One for Kids by Ryan Sheehy

The Coach ADVenture by Amy Illingworth

Creatively Productive by Lisa Johnson

The Ed Branding Book by Dr. Renae Bryant and Lynette White

Educational Eye Exam by Alicia Ray

The EduNinja Mindset by Jennifer Burdis

Empower Our Girls by Lynmara Colón and Adam Welcome

Finding Lifelines by Andrew Grieve and Andrew Sharos

The Four O'Clock Faculty by Rich Czyz

How Much Water Do We Have? by Pete and Kris Nunweiler

P Is for Pirate by Dave and Shelley Burgess

A Passion for Kindness by Tamara Letter

The Path to Serendipity by Allyson Apsey

PheMOMenal Teacher by Annick Rauch

Recipes for Resilience by Robert A. Martinez

Rogue Leader by Rich Czyz

Sanctuaries by Dan Tricarico

Saving Sycamore by Molly B. Hudgens

The Secret Sauce by Rich Czyz

Shattering the Perfect Teacher Myth by Aaron Hogan

Stories from Webb by Todd Nesloney

Talk to Me by Kim Bearden

Teach Better by Chad Ostrowski, Tiffany Ott, Rae Hughart, and Jeff Gargas

Teach Me, Teacher by Jacob Chastain

Teach, Play, Learn! by Adam Peterson

The Teachers of Oz by Herbie Raad and Nathan Lang-Raad

Teaching Is a Tattoo by Mike Johnston

Teaching the Ms. Abbott Way by Joyce Stephens Abbott

TeamMakers by Laura Robb and Evan Robb

Through the Lens of Serendipity by Allyson Apsey

Write Here and Now by Dan Tricarico

The Zen Teacher by Dan Tricarico

Children's Books

The Adventures of Little Mickey by Mickey Smith Jr.

Alpert by LaNesha Tabb

Alpert & Friends by LaNesha Tabb

Beyond Us by Aaron Polansky

Cannonball In by Tara Martin

Dolphins in Trees by Aaron Polansky

Dragon Smart by Tisha and Tommy Richmond

I Can Achieve Anything by MoNique Waters

I Want to Be a Lot by Ashley Savage

The Magic of Wonder by Jenna Copper, Ashley Bible, Abby Gross, and Staci Lamb

Micah's Big Question by Naomi O'Brien

The Princes of Serendip by Allyson Apsey

Ride with Emilio by Richard Nares

A Teacher's Top Secret Confidential by LaNesha Tabb

A Teacher's Top Secret: Mission Accomplished by LaNesha Tabb

The Wild Card Kids by Hope and Wade King

Zom-Be a Design Thinker by Amanda Fox

www.ingramcontent.com/pod-product-compliance
Lightning Source LLC
Chambersburg PA
CBHW050520170426
43201CB00013B/2027